ROUGH GUIDES **PHRASEBOOK**

FRENCH

ROUGH
GUIDES

Contacting the Editors

Every effort has been made to provide accurate information in this publication, but changes are inevitable. The publisher cannot be responsible for any resulting loss, inconvenience or injury.
We would appreciate it if readers would call our attention to any errors or outdated information. We also welcome your suggestions; if you come across a relevant expression not in our phrase book, please contact us at: **mail@uk.roughguides.com**

Cover & Interior Design: Slawomir Krajewski
Head of Production: Rebeka Davies
Production Manager: Rebecca Hancock
Picture Researcher: Slawomir Krajewski
Cover Photo: all shutterstock

Interior Photos: all shutterstock

CONTENTS

INTRODUCTION

Pronunciation	7	Grammar	12
How to use the App	10		

PRACTICALITIES

THE BASICS	**20**	NEED TO KNOW	29
NUMBERS	**20**	Border Control	30
NEED TO KNOW	20	**MONEY**	**31**
Ordinal Numbers	22	NEED TO KNOW	31
TIME	**23**	At the Bank	32
NEED TO KNOW	23	**CONVERSATION**	**34**
DAYS	**24**	NEED TO KNOW	34
NEED TO KNOW	24	Language Difficulties	35
Dates	25	Making Friends	37
Months	26	Travel Talk	38
Seasons	26	Personal	38
Holidays	27	Work & School	40
ARRIVAL & DEPARTURE	**29**	Weather	41

ON THE WAY

GETTING AROUND	**44**	Taxi	59
NEED TO KNOW	44	Bicycle & Motorbike	62
Tickets	45	Car Hire	62
Airport Transfer	47	Fuel Station	64
Checking In	50	Asking Directions	64
Luggage	52	Parking	67
Finding your Way	52	Breakdown & Repair	68
Train	53	Accidents	68
Departures	55	**PLACES TO STAY**	**69**
On Board	56	NEED TO KNOW	69
Bus	56	Somewhere to Stay	70
Metro	57	At the Hotel	71
Boat & Ferry	58	Price	73

Preferences 74
Questions 74
Problems 76
Checking Out 77
Renting 78
Domestic Items 80
At the Hostel 81
Going Camping 83
COMMUNICATIONS **84**
NEED TO KNOW 84
Online 86

Social Media 88
Phone 90
Telephone Etiquette 92
Fax 94
Post 94
SIGHTSEEING **96**
NEED TO KNOW 96
Tourist Information 96
On Tour 97
Seeing the Sights 98
Religious Sites 101

LEISURE TIME

SHOPPING **104**
NEED TO KNOW 104
At the Shops 105
Ask an Assistant 106
Personal Preferences 108
Paying & Bargaining 109
Making a Complaint 110
Services 111
Hair & Beauty 112
Antiques 114
Clothing 114
Colors 116
Clothes & Accessories 117
Fabric 119
Shoes 120
Sizes 120

Newsstand & Tobacconist 121
Photography 122
Souvenirs 123
SPORT & LEISURE **126**
NEED TO KNOW 126
Watching Sport 127
Playing Sport 128
At the Beach/Pool 129
Winter Sports 132
Out in the Country 133
TRAVELING
WITH CHILDREN **136**
NEED TO KNOW 136
Out & About 137
Baby Essentials 138
Babysitting 139

SAFE TRAVEL

EMERGENCIES **142**
NEED TO KNOW 142
POLICE **144**
NEED TO KNOW 144
Crime & Lost Property 145
HEALTH **146**

NEED TO KNOW 146
Finding a Doctor 147
Symptoms 147
Conditions 150
Treatment 151
Hospital 151

Dentist	152	Basic Supplies	157
Gynecologist	152	Child Health &	
Optician	153	Emergency	159
Payment & Insurance	153	**DISABLED TRAVELERS**	**160**
PHARMACY	**154**	NEED TO KNOW	160
NEED TO KNOW	154	Asking for Assistance	160
What to Take	155		

FOOD

EATING OUT	**164**	Meat & Poultry	183
NEED TO KNOW	164	Vegetables & Staples	185
Where to Eat	165	Fruit	188
Reservations &		Cheese	189
Preferences	166	Dessert	190
How to Order	168	Sauces & Condiments	192
Cooking Methods	170	At the Market	193
Dietary Requirements	171	In the Kitchen	195
Dining with Children	172	**DRINKS**	**197**
How to Complain	173	NEED TO KNOW	197
Paying	173	Non-alcoholic Drinks	198
MEALS & COOKING	**175**	Aperitifs, Cocktails &	
Breakfast	175	Liqueurs	200
Appetizers	177	Beer	201
Soup	179	Wine	201
Fish & Seafood	181	**ON THE MENU**	**204**

PEOPLE

GOING OUT	**224**	NEED TO KNOW	228
NEED TO KNOW	224	The Dating Game	228
Entertainment	225	Accepting & Rejecting	230
Nightlife	226	Getting Intimate	230
ROMANCE	**228**	Sexual Preferences	231

DICTIONARY

ENGLISH–FRENCH	**234**	**FRENCH–ENGLISH**	**258**

PRONUNCIATION

This section is designed to make you familiar with the sounds of French using our simplified phonetic transcription. You'll find the pronunciation of the French letters and sounds explained below, together with their 'imitated' equivalents. This system is used throughout the phrase book; simply read the pronunciation as if it were English, noting any special rules below.

In French, all syllables are pronounced the same, with no extra stress on any particular syllable. The French language contains nasal vowels, which are indicated in the pronunciation by a vowel symbol followed by an **N**. This **N** should not be pronounced strongly, but it is there to show the nasal quality of the previous vowel. A nasal vowel is pronounced simultaneously through the mouth and the nose.

In French, the final consonants of words are not always pronounced. When a word ending in a consonant is followed with a word beginning with a vowel, the two words are often run together. The consonant is therefore pronounced as if it begins the following word.

Example	Pronunciation
comment	*koh • mawN*
Comment allez-vous ?	*koh • mawN tah • lay-voo*

CONSONANTS

Letter	Approximate Pronunciation	Symbol	Example	Pronunciation
cc	1. before, e, i, like cc in accident	**ks**	**accessible**	*ahk • seh • see • bluh*
	2. elsewhere, like cc in accommodate	**k**	**d'accord**	*dah • kohr*
ch	like sh in shut	**sh**	**chercher**	*shehr • shay*
ç	like s in sit	**s**	**ça**	*sah*

Letter	Approximate Pronunciation	Symbol	Example	Pronunciation
g	1. before e, i, y, like s in pleasure	zh	**manger**	*mawN•zhay*
	2. before a, o, u, like g in go	g	**garçon**	*gahr•sohN*
h	always silent		**homme**	*ohm*
j	like s in pleasure	zh	**jamais**	*zhah•may*
qu	like k in kill	k	**qui**	*kee*
r	rolled in the back of the, like gargling	r	**rouge**	*roozh*
w	usually like v in voice	v	**wagon**	*vah•gohN*

B, c, d, f, k, l, m, n, p, s, t, v, x and z are pronounced as in English.

VOWELS

Letter	Approximate Pronunciation	Symbol	Example	Pronunciation
a, à, â	like a in father a in hat and the a in father	ah	**mari**	*mah•ree*
e	sometimes like	uh	**je**	*zhuh*
è, ê, e	like e in get	eh	**même**	*mehm*
é, ez	like a in late	ay	**été**	*ay•tay*
i	like ee in meet	ee	**il**	*eel*
o, ô	generally like o in roll	oh	**donner**	*doh•nay*
u	like ew in dew	oo	**une**	*ewn*

SOUNDS SPELLED WITH TWO OR MORE LETTERS

Letter	Approximate Pronunciation	Symbol	Example	Pronunciation
ai, ay, aient, ais, ait	like a in late	**ay**	**j'ai**	*zhay*
aî, ei	like e in get	**eh**	**chaîne** **peine**	*shehn* *pehn*
(e)au	similar to o	**oh**	**chaud**	*shoh*
eu, eû, œu	like u in fur but short like a puff of air	**uh**	**euro**	*uh•roh*
euil, euille	like uh + y	**uhy**	**feuille**	*fuhy*
ail, aille	like ie in tie	**ie**	**taille**	*tie*
ille	1. like yu in yucca 2. like eel	**eeyuh** **eel**	**famille** **ville**	*fah-meeyuh* *veel*
oi, oy	like w followed by the a in hat	**wah**	**moi**	*mwah*
ou, oû	like o in move or oo in hoot	**oo**	**nouveau**	*noo•voh*
ui	approximately wee in between	**wee**	**traduire**	*trah•dweer*

There are approximately 129 million French speakers worldwide. French is an official language in 30 countries and the United Nations. French is spoken by 4 million people in Belgium, 7 million in Canada, 60.5 million in France and 1.3 million in Switzerland. It is also an official language of 22 African nations.

HOW TO USE THE APP

Quickly access your recently viewed entries

Look up words and phrases on-the-go

Conveniently navigate the phrasebook categories

Change font size and background color

Save the most useful everyday words and phrases to your Favorites

Use the Flash Cards Quiz to learn and memorize new words easily

Take all digital advantages of the app: listen to words and phrases pronounced by native speakers

To learn how to Activate the app, see the inside back cover of this phrasebook.

GRAMMAR

REGULAR VERBS

Regular French verbs follow a set pattern for conjugation. Remove the **-er**, **-ir** or **-re** ending and replace it with the correct ending for the tense and gender. See the tables below for examples of regular **-er**, **-ir** and **-re** verbs and the appropriate endings (in bold).

French uses subject pronouns (I, you, he, etc.) in much the same ways as English does. The first-person singular subject pronoun (I) is **je**. **Je** is abbreviated to **j'** if the following word begins with a vowel.

PARLER		PRESENT	PAST	FUTURE
I	je/j'	parle	ai parlé	parlerai
you (sing.)	tu	parles	as parlé	parleras
he/she	il *m*/elle *f*	parle	a parlé	parlera
we	nous	parlons	avons parlé	parlerons
you (pl.)	vous	parlez	avez parlé	parlerez
they	ils *m*/ elles *f*	parlent	ont parlé	parleront

CHOISIR		PRESENT	PAST	FUTURE
I	je/j'	choisis	ai choisi	choisirai
you (sing.)	tu	choisis	as choisi	choisiras
he/she	il *m*/elle *f*	choisit	a choisi	choisira
we	nous	choisissons	avons choisi	choisirons
you (pl.)	vous	choisissez	avez choisi	choisirez
they	ils *m*/ elles *f*	choisissent	ont choisi	choisiront

ATTENDRE		PRESENT	PAST	FUTURE
I	je/j'	attends	ai attendu	*attendrai*
you (sing.)	tu	attends	as attendu	*attendras*
he/she	il *m*/elle *f*	attend	a attendu	*attendra*
we	nous	attendons	avons attendu	*choisirons*
you (pl.)	vous	attendez	avez attendu	*attendrez*
they	ils *m*/ elles *f*	attendent	ont attendu	*attendrent*

IRREGULAR VERBS

There are many irregular verbs that do not follow the standard conjugation rules and must be memorized. Two common irregular verbs are **avoir** (to have) and **être** (to be). **Avoir** and **être** are used as auxiliary verbs in the past tense. Most verbs use **avoir**, but several common, important verbs use **être**. In general, verbs of coming and going use **être** in the past tense, e.g., **aller** (to go), **venir** (to come), **sortir** (to go out), **partir** (to leave) and **arriver** (to arrive).

AVOIR (TO HAVE)	
I have	j'ai
you (sing.) have	tu as
he/she has	il *m*/elle *f* a
we have	nous avons
you (pl.) have	vous avez
they have	ils *m*/elles *f* ont

ÊTRE (TO BE)	
I am	je suis
you (sing.) are	tu es
he/she is	il *m*/elle *f* est
we are	nous sommes
you (pl.) are	vous êtes
they are	ils *m*/elles *f* sont

WORD ORDER

French sentences are constructed as in English: subject, verb, object.
Example: **Nous achetons un livre.** We're buying a book.
Questions can be formed in four different ways. The easiest is to just raise your voice at the end of a sentence:
Vous parlez anglais? You speak English?
You can also add **n'est-ce pas** (isn't that so/right) at the end of a phrase:
Vous parlez anglais, n'est-ce pas? You speak English, right?
You can put **est-ce que** in front of a phrase:
Est-ce que vous parlez anglais? Do you speak English?
You can also put the verb before the subject:
Parlez-vous anglais? Do you speak English?
(literally: Speak you English?)

NEGATIONS

Negative sentences are generally formed by adding **ne** before the verb and **pas** after it. When spoken, the ne is often dropped.
Example: **Nous fumons.** We smoke.
Nous ne fumons pas. We do not smoke.

IMPERATIVES

Most imperatives are formed by using the stem of the verb with the appropriate ending.

you (sing.)	tu	**Parle!** Wait!	**Attends!** Speak!
we	nous	**Parlons!** Let's speak!	**Attendons!** Let's wait!
you (pl.)	vous	**Parlez!** Speak!	**Attendez!** Wait!

NOUNS & ARTICLES

In French, nouns are either masculine or feminine. The singular definite articles (the) are **le**, for masculine nouns, and **la**, for feminine nouns.
Les is the plural definite article for both masculine and feminine nouns.
Generally, nouns ending in **-e**, **-té** and **-tion** are feminine and take **la**.

Gender	Singular		Plural	
masculine	**un train**	a train	**des trains**	trains
feminine	**une table**	a table	**des tables**	tables

ADJECTIVES

Adjectives describe nouns and must agree with the noun in gender and number. To form the feminine of many common adjectives, add **-e** to the masculine; if the word already ends in **-e** there is no change. To form the plural adjective, add **-s** to the end; if the word already ends in **-s** there is no change.
Examples:

un livre intéressant	an interesting book
des livres intéresssants	interesting books
une fille intéressante	an interesting girl
des filles intéressantes	interesting girls

COMPARATIVES & SUPERLATIVES

Comparatives are formed by adding **plus** (more) or **moins** (less) before the adjective. Superlatives are formed by adding **le _m_/la _f_ plus** (most) or **le _m_/la _f_ moins** (least) before the adjective.
Examples:

le vin sec	the dry wine
le vin plus sec	the drier wine

le vin le plus sec	the driest wine
la bague chère	the expensive ring
la bague moins chère	the less expensive ring
la bague la moins chère	the least expensive ring

POSSESSIVE ADJECTIVES

Possessive adjectives come before the noun and must agree in gender and number with the noun/object, not the person possessing the object.

	Masculine	Feminine	Plural
my	**mon**	**ma**	**mes**
your (sing.)	**ton**	**ta**	**tes**
his/her	**son**	**sa**	**ses**
our	**notre**	**notre**	**nos**
your (pl.)	**votre**	**votre**	**vos**
their	**leur**	**leur**	**leurs**

Example:

Où sont nos passeports? Cherchons dans mon sac et dans ta valise.

Where are our passports? Let's look in my purse and in your suitcase.

ADVERBS & ADVERBIAL EXPRESSIONS

Adverbs describe verbs. They are often formed by adding **-ment** to the feminine form of the adjective.

Examples:

Nous prenons le train lent.	We are taking the slow train.
Jean conduit lentement.	Jean drives slowly.
Il prends la route rapide.	He is taking the fast route.
Frédérique conduit rapidement.	Frédérique drives fast.

PREPOSITIONS

Prepositions are paired with nouns or verbs to create descriptive phrases. In French, several important prepositions form contractions when they appear in front of certain other words.

SOME/ANY

To express how much of something (to eat, to buy, etc.), French uses a construction called the partitive. The partitive is similar to some or any in English, and it is formed by combining **de** with the definite article (**le**, **la** or **les**). Even if some or any is not explicit in English, the partitive is always used in French.
Examples:

de + la *f* (sing.) = de la	**Je voudrais de la soupe.**
	I'd like some soup.
de + le *m* (sing.) = du	**Avez-vous commandé du fromage?**
	Did you order any cheese?
de + l' (before a vowel = de l'	**Nous avons commandé de l'eau.**
	We have ordered some water.
de + les (pl.) = des	**Il achete des chaussures.**
	He is buying shoes.

AT/TO

French expressions that use the word à are formed somewhat like the phrases using de.
Examples:

à + la *f* (sing.) = à la	**Je vais à la plage.**
	I'm going to the beach.
à + le *m* (sing.) = au	**Nous restons au musée.**
	We're staying at the museum.
à + l' (before a vowel = à l'	**Elles sont à l'église.**
	They are at the church.
à + les (pl.) = aux	**Ils vont aux États-Unis.**
	They are going to the United States.

PRACTICALITIES

THE BASICS   20

ARRIVAL & DEPARTURE   29

MONEY   31

CONVERSATION   34

THE BASICS

NUMBERS

NEED TO KNOW

0	**zéro**
	zay•roh
1	**un**
	uhN
2	**deux**
	duh
3	**trois**
	trwah
4	**quatre**
	kah•truh
5	**cinq**
	sehNk
6	**six**
	sees
7	**sept**
	seht
8	**huit**
	weet
9	**neuf**
	nuhf
10	**dix**
	dees
11	**onze**
	ohNz
12	**douze**
	dooz

13	**treize**
	trehz
14	**quatorze**
	kah • tohrz
15	**quinze**
	kehNz
16	**seize**
	sehz
17	**dix-sept**
	dee • seht
18	**dix-huit**
	deez • weet
19	**dix-neuf**
	deez • nuhf
20	**vingt**
	vehN
21	**vingt-et-un**
	vehN • tay • uhN
22	**vingt-deux**
	vehN • duh
30	**trente**
	trawNt
31	**trente-et-un**
	trawN • tay • uhN
40	**quarante**
	kah • rawNt
50	**cinquante**
	sehN • kawNt
60	**soixante**
	swah • zawNt
70	**soixante-dix**
	swah • zawNt • dees

80	**quatre-vingt**
	kah • truh • vehN
90	**quatre-vingt-dix**
	kah • truh • vehN • dees
100	**cent**
	sawN
101	**cent-un**
	sawN • uhN
200	**deux-cent**
	duh • sawN
500	**cinq-cent**
	sehNk • sawN
1,000	**mille**
	meel
10,000	**dix mille**
	dee meel
1,000,000	**un million**
	uhN meel • yohN

ORDINAL NUMBERS

first	**premier** *m*/**première** *f*
	pruh • meeyay/pruh • meeyehr
second	**deuxième**
	duh • zeeyehm
third	**troisième**
	trwah • zeeyehm
fourth	**quatrième**
	kah • treeyehm
fifth	**cinquième**
	sehN • keeyehm

once	**une fois**
	ewn fwah
twice	**deux fois**
	duh fwah
three times	**trois fois**
	trwah fwah

TIME

NEED TO KNOW

What time is it?	**Quelle heure est-il ?**
	kehl uhr ay • teel
It's midday.	**Il est midi.**
	ee lay mee • dee
At midnight.	**À minuit.**
	ah mee • nwee
From one o'clock to two o'clock.	**D'une heure à deux heures.**
	dewn nuhr ah duh zuhr
Five past three.	**Trois heures cinq.**
	trwah zuhr sehNk
A quarter to ten.	**Dix heures moins le quart.**
	dee zuhr mwehN luh kahr
5:30 a.m./p.m.	**Cinq heures et demie du matin/ de l'après-midi.**
	sehN kuhr eh duh • mee dew mah • tehN/ • duh lah • preh mee • dee

In France, the 24-hour clock is used for time, especially in schedules. The morning hours from 1:00 a.m. to noon are the same as in English.
After that, just add 12 to the time: 1:00 p.m. would be 13:00, 5:00 p.m. would be 17:00 and so on. In ordinary conversation, time is generally expressed using the 12-hour clock, with the addition of **du matin** (morning/a.m.), **de l'après-midi** (afternoon) or **du soir** (evening/p.m.).

DAYS

NEED TO KNOW

Monday	**lundi**	
	luhN • dee	
Tuesday	**mardi**	
	mahr • dee	
Wednesday	**mercredi**	
	mehr • kruh • dee	
Thursday	**jeudi**	
	zhuh • dee	
Friday	**vendredi**	
	vawN • druh • dee	
Saturday	**samedi**	
	sahm • dee	
Sunday	**dimanche**	
	dee • mawNsh	

Calendars in France are organized Monday to Sunday.

DATES

yesterday	**hier**
	eeyehr
today	**aujourd'hui**
	oh • zhoor • dwee
tomorrow	**demain**
	duh • mehN
day	**le jour**
	luh zhoor
week	**la semaine**
	lah suh • mehN
month	**le mois**
	luh mwah
year	**l'année/l'an**
	lah • nay/lawN

France follows a day-month-year format instead of the month-day-year format used in the U.S.
E.g.: **le vingt-cinq juillet deux mille huit** = July 25, 2008;
25/07/08 = 7/25/2008

MONTHS

January	**janvier**
	zhawN • veeyay
February	**février**
	fay • vreeyay
March	**mars**
	mahrs
April	**avril**
	ah • vreel
May	**mai**
	may
June	**juin**
	zhwehN
July	**juillet**
	zhwee • yay
August	**août**
	oot
September	**septembre**
	sehp • tawN • bruh
October	**octobre**
	ohk • toh • bruh
November	**novembre**
	noh • vawN • bruh
December	**décembre**
	day • sawN • bruh

SEASONS

spring	**le printemps**
	luh prehN • tawN
summer	**l'été**
	lay • tay

autumn	**l'automne**
	loh • tohNn
winter	**l'hiver**
	lee • vehr

HOLIDAYS

January 1: New Year's Day, **Le Nouvel An**
May 1: Labor Day, **La Fête du Travail**
May 8: Victory Day, **La Fête de la Libération**
July 14: Bastille Day, **La Fête Nationale**
August 15: Assumption Day, **L'Assomption**
November 1: All Saints Day, **La Toussaint**
November 11: Armistice Day, **L'Armistice**
December 25: Christmas, **Noël**
Good Friday, **Le Vendredi Saint**
Easter, **Pâques**
Easter Monday, **Le Lundi de Pâques**
Ascension, **L'Ascension**
Pentecost, **La Pentecôte**

The most important public holiday is **La Fête Nationale** (Bastille Day) on July 14. This holiday symbolizes the victory of the revolutionaries over the monarchy in 1789, creating the basis for the French Republic.

La Marseillaise, the French national anthem, was created during the French Revolution, along with France's motto: **Liberté, Égalité, Fraternité** (Liberty, Equality, Brotherhood). The evening before July 14, people go to cafes and improvised dance areas; it is a festive atmosphere with dancing and celebration. There are firework displays throughout France that evening and on the 14th. The French president and members of the government, as well as other dignitaries, attend the **défilé**, a large military parade, on the Champs Élysées on Bastille Day.

ARRIVAL & DEPARTURE

NEED TO KNOW

I'm on vacation [holiday]/business.
Je suis en vacances/voyage d'affaires.
zhuh swee zawN vah•kawNs/ vwah•yahzh dah•fehr

I'm going to…
Je vais à/aux…
zhuh vay ah/oh…

I'm staying at … the…Hotel.
Je reste à l'hôtel…
zhuh rehst ah loh•tehl…

YOU MAY HEAR…

Votre passeport, s'il vous plaît.
voh•truh pahs•pohr seel voo play
Your passport, please.

Quel est le but de votre visite ?
keh lay luh bewt duh voh•truh vee•zeet
What's the purpose of your visit?

Où restez-vous ?
oo rehs•tay•voo
Where are you staying?

Combien de temps restez-vous ?
kohN•beeyehN duh tawN rehs•tay•voo
How long are you staying?

Avec qui êtes-vous ?
ah•vehk kee eht•voo
Who are you here with?

BORDER CONTROL

I'm just passing through.	**Je suis juste en transit.** *zhuh swee zhews tawN trawN • zeet*
I'd like to declare…	**Je voudrais déclarer…** *zhuh voo • dray day • klah • ray…*
I have nothing to declare.	**Je n'ai rien à déclarer.** *zhuh nay reeyehN nah day • klah • ray*

YOU MAY HEAR…

Rien à déclarer ?
reeyehN nah day • klah • ray

Anything to declare?

Vous devez payer la taxe sur ceci.
voo duh • vay pay • yay lah tahks sewr suh • see

You must pay duty on this.

Ouvrez ce sac.
oo • vray suh sahk

Open this bag.

YOU MAY SEE…

DOUANES	customs
ARTICLES HORS TAXES	duty-free goods
PRODUITS À DÉCLARER	goods to declare
RIEN À DÉCLARER	nothing to declare
CONTRÔLE DE PASSEPORT	passport control
POLICE	police

MONEY

NEED TO KNOW

Where's...?	**Où est...?**
	oo ay...
the ATM	**le distributeur automatique de billets**
	luh dee • stree • bew • tuhr oh • toh • mah • teek duh bee • yay
the bank	**la banque**
	lah bawNk
the currency exchange office	**le bureau de change**
	luh bew • roh duh shawNzh
When does the bank open/close?	**Quand est-ce que la banque ouvre/ ferme ?**
	kawN tehs kuh lah bawNk oo • vruh/ fehrm
I'd like to change dollars/pounds into euros.	**Je voudrais échanger des dollars/ livres sterling en euros.**
	zhuh voo • dray ay • shawN • zhay day doh • lahr/lee • vruh stayr • leeng awN nuh • roh
I'd like to cash traveler's cheques.	**Je voudrais encaisser des chèques de voyages.**
	zhuh voo • dray awN • kay • say day shehk duh vwah • yahzh

AT THE BANK

I'd like to change money/get a cash advance.	**Je voudrais changer de l'argent/obtenir une avance en liquide.** *zhuh voo • dray shawN • zhay duh lahr • zhawN/ohb • tuh • neer ewn ah • vawNs awN lee • keed*
What's the exchange rate/fee?	**Quel est le taux de/prix du change ?** *keh lay luh toh duh/pree dew shawNzh*
I think there's mistake.	**Je pense qu'il y a une erreur.** *zhuh pawNs a keel • yah ewn ay • ruhr*
I lost my traveler's cheques.	**J'ai perdu mes chèques de voyages.** *zhay pehr • dew may shehk duh vwah • yahzh*
The ATM ate my card.	**Le distributeur automatique de billets a avalé ma carte.** *luh dee • stree • bew • tuhr oh • toh • mah • teek duh bee • yay ah ah • vah • lay mah kahrt*
My card...	**Ma carte...** *mah kahrt...*
was lost	**a été perdue** *ah ay • tay pehr • dew*
was stolen	**a été volée** *ah ay • tay voh • lay*
doesn't work	**ne fonctionne pas** *nuh fohNk • seeyohn pah*

For Numbers, see page 20.

YOU MAY SEE...

INSÉREZ LA CARTE ICI	insert card here
ANNULER	cancel
EFFACER	clear
VALIDER	enter
CODE SECRET	PIN
RETRAIT	withdrawal
DU COMPTE COURANT	from checking [current] account
DU COMPTE ÉPARGNE	from savings
REÇU	receipt

Cash can be obtained from ATMs with Visa™, Eurocard™, American Express® and many other international cards. Instructions are often given in English. Banks with a **Change** sign will exchange foreign currency. You can also change money at travel agencies and hotels, but the rate will not be as good. Remember to bring your passport when you want to change money.

YOU MAY SEE...

The French currency is the **euro**, **€**, which is divided into 100 **cents**.
Coins: 1, 2, 5, 10, 20 and 50 **cents**; €1, 2
Bills: €5, 10, 20, 50, 100, 200 and 500

CONVERSATION

NEED TO KNOW

Hello!/Hi!	**Bonjour !/Salut !**
	bohN • zhoor/sah • lew
How are you?	**Comment allez-vous ?**
	koh • mawN tah • lay • voo
Fine, thanks.	**Bien, merci.**
	beeyehN mehr • see
Excuse me!	**Excusez-moi !**
	ehk • skew • zay • mwah
Do you speak	**Parlez-vous anglais ?**
	pahr • lay • voo zawN • glay English?
What's your name?	**Comment vous appelez-vous ?**
	koh • mawN voo zah • puh • lay • voo
My name is…	**Je m'appelle…**
	zhuh mah • pehl…
Nice to meet you.	**Enchanté m /Enchantée f.**
	awN • shawN • tay
Where are you from?	**D'où êtes-vous ?**
	doo eht • voo
I'm from the U.K./U.S.	**Je viens du Royaume-Uni/des États-Unis.**
	zhuh veeyehN dew rwah • yohm • ew • nee/day zay • tah • zew • nee
What do you do for a living?	**Que faites-vous dans la vie ?**
	kuh feht • voo dawN lah vee
I work for…	**Je travaille pour…**
	zhuh trah • vie poor…

I'm a student.	**Je suis étudiant** *m*/**étudiante** *f*.
	zhuh swee zay • tew • deeyawN/
	zay • tew • deeyawnt
I'm retired.	**Je suis à la retraite.**
	zhuh swee zah lah ruh • trayt
Do you like…?	**Aimez-vous…?**
	eh • may • voo…
Goodbye.	**Au revôir.**
	oh ruh • vwahr
See you later.	**À bientôt.**
	ah beeyehN • toh

When addressing someone, it is polite to include a title: **monsieur** for a man or **madame** for a woman, even if you suspect she is not married. **Mademoiselle** is used only when addressing young girls.

LANGUAGE DIFFICULTIES

Do you speak English?	**Parlez-vous anglais ?**
	pahr • lay • voo zawN • glay
Does anyone here speak English?	**Est-ce que quelqu'un parle anglais ici ?**
	ehs kuh kehl • kuhN pahrl awN • glay
	ee • see
I don't speak (much) French.	**Je ne parle pas (bien le) français.**
	zhuh nuh pahrl pah (beeyehN luh)
	frawN • say

Can you speak more slowly?	**Pouvez-vous parler plus lentement ?** *poo • vay • voo pahr • lay plew lawN • tuh • mawN*
Can you repeat that?	**Pouvez-vous répéter ?** *poo • vay • voo ray • pay • tay*
Excuse me?	**Excusez-moi ?** *ehk • skew • zay • mwah*
Can you spell it?	**Pouvez-vous l'épeler ?** *poo • vay • voo lay • puh • lay*
Can you write it down?	**S'il vous plaît, écrivez-le.** *seel voo play ay • kree • vay • luh*
Can you translate this into English for me?	**Pouvez-vous traduire ceci en anglais pour moi ?** *poo • vay • voo trah • dweer suh • see awN nawN • glay poor mwah*
What does this/that mean?	**Qu'est ce que ceci/cela veut dire ?** *kehs kuh suh • see/suh • lah vuh deer*
I understand.	**Je comprends.** *zhuh kohN • prawN*
I don't understand.	**Je ne comprends pas.** *zhuh nuh kohN • prawN pah*
Do you understand?	**Comprenez-vous ?** *kohN • pruh • nay • voo*

YOU MAY HEAR...

Je parle un peu anglais.
zhuh pahrl uhN puh awN • glay
Je ne parle pas anglais.
zhuh nuh pahrl pah zawN • glay

I only speak a little English.
I don't speak English.

MAKING FRIENDS

Hello!	**Bonjour !** *bohN • zhoor*
Good afternoon.	**Bon après-midi.** *bohN nah • pray • mee • dee*
Good evening.	**Bonsoir.** *bohN • swahr*
My name is…	**Je m'appelle…** *zhuh mah • pehl…*
What's your name?	**Comment vous appelez-vous ?** *koh • mawN voo zah • puh • lay • voo*
I'd like to introduce you to…	**Je voudrais vous présenter…** *zhuh voo • dray voo pray • zawN • tay…*
Pleased to meet you.	**Enchanté** *m*/ **Enchantée** *f*. *awN • shawN • tay*
How are you?	**Comment allez-vous ?** *koh • mawN tah • lay • voo*
Fine, thanks. And you?	**Bien, merci. Et vous ?** *beeyehN mehr • see ay voo*

In France, people greet each other with a firm handshake on first meeting. Once they become more familiar, people give from one to four or more kisses (cheek-to-cheek contact). Cheek-kissing among men, however, is usually reserved for family members and close friends.

TRAVEL TALK

I'm here…	**Je suis ici…**
	zhuh swee zee • see…
on business	**pour les affaires**
	poor lay zah • fehr
on vacation [holiday]	**en vacances**
	awN vah • kawNs
studying	**pour étudier**
	poor ay • tew • deeyay
I'm staying for…	**Je reste pour…**
	zhuh rehst poor…
I've been here…	**Je suis ici depuis…**
	zhuh swee zee • see duh • pwee…
a day	**un jour**
	uhN zhoor
a week	**une semaine**
	ewn suh • mehN
a month	**un mois**
	uhN mwah
Where are you from?	**D'où êtes-vous ?**
	doo eht • voo
I'm from…	**Je suis de…**
	zhuh swee duh…

PERSONAL

Who are you with?	**Avec qui êtes-vous ?**
	ah • vehk kee eht • voo
I'm here alone.	**Je suis seul** *m*/**seule** *f.*
	zhuh swee suhl
I'm with…	**Je suis avec…**
	zhuh swee zah • vehk…

my husband/wife	**mon mari** m/**ma femme** f.
	mohN mah•ree/mah fahm
my boyfriend/ girlfriend	**mon petit-ami** m/**ma petite-amie** f
	mawN puh•tee•tah•mee/mah puh•tee•tah•mee
a friend	**un ami** m/**une amie** f
	uhN nah•mee/ewn ah•mee
friends	**des amis**
	day zah•mee
a colleague	**un collègue** m/**une collègue** f
	uhN koh•lehg /ewn koh•lehg
colleagues	**des collègues**
	day koh•lehg
When's your birthday?	**Quand est votre anniversaire ?**
	kawN teh voh•truh ah•nee•vehr•sehr
How old are you?	**Quel âge avez-vous ?**
	keh lahzh ah•vay•voo
I'm…	**J'ai…ans.**
	zhay…awN
Are you married?	**Êtes-vous marié** m/**mariée** f **?**
	eht•voo mah•reeay
I'm…	**Je suis…**
	zhuh swee…
single/in a relationship	**célibataire/en ménage**
	say•lee•bah•tehr/ awN may•nahzh
engaged	**fiancé** m/**fiancée** f
	feeyawN•say
married	**marié** m/**mariée** f
	mah•reeay
divorced	**divorcé** m/**divorcée** f
	dee•vohr•say
separated	**séparé** m/**séparée** f
	say•pah•ray
widowed	**veuf** m/**veuve** f
	vuhf/vuhv

Do you have children/ grandchildren?	**Avez-vous des enfants/petits-enfants ?** *ah • vay • voo day zawN • fawN/ puh • tee • zawN • fawN*

For Numbers, see page 20.

WORK & SCHOOL

What do you do for a living?	**Que faites-vous dans la vie ?** *kuh feht • voo dawN lah vee*
What are you studying?	**Qu'étudiez-vous ?** *kay • tew • deeyay • voo*
I'm studying French.	**J'étudie le français.** *zhay • tew • dee luh frawN • say*
I...	**Je...** *zhuh...*
work full-/ part-time	**travaille à temps plein/partiel** *trah • vie ah tawN plehN/pahr • syehl*
am unemployed	**suis au chômage** *swee zoh shoh • mahzh*
work at home	**travaille à la maison** *trah • vie ah lah may • zohN*
Who do you work for?	**Pour qui travaillez-vous ?** *poor kee trah • vie • yay • voo*
I work for...	**Je travaille pour...** *zhuh trah • vie poor...*
Here's my business card.	**Voici ma carte de visite.** *vwah • see mah kahrt duh vee • zeet*

For Communications, see page 84.

WEATHER

What's the forecast?	**Que dit la météo ?**
	kuh dee lah may • tay • oh
What beautiful/	**Quel beau/terrible temps !**
terrible weather!	*kehl boh/teh • ree • bluh tawN*
It's…	**Il fait…**
	Eel fay…
cool/warm	**frais/chaud**
	fray/shoh
cold/hot	**froid/très chaud**
	frwah/tray shoh
rainy/sunny	**pluvieux/ensoleillé**
	plew • veeyuh/awN • soh • lehyay
snowy/icy	**enneigé/gelé**
	awN • neh • zhay/zheh • lay
Do I need a	**Ai-je besoin d'une veste/d'un parapluie?**
jacket/an umbrella?	*ay • zhuh buh • zwehN dewn vehst/duhN*
	pah • rah • plewee

For Months, see page 26.

ON THE WAY

GETTING AROUND 44

PLACES TO STAY   69

COMMUNICATIONS

84

SIGHTSEEING   96

GETTING AROUND

NEED TO KNOW

How do I get to town?	**Comment vais-je en ville ?** *koh • mawN vay • zhuh awN veel*
Where's…?	**Où est…?** *oo ay…*
the airport	**l'aéroport** *lah • ay • roh • pohr*
the train station	**la gare** *lah gahr*
the bus station	**la gare routière** *lah gahr roo • tee • yehr*
the Metro station	**le métro** *luh may • troh*
Is it far from here?	**C'est loin d'ici ?** *say lwehN dee • see*
Where do I buy a ticket?	**Où puis-je acheter un billet ?** *oo pwee • zhuh a ah shtay uhN bee • yay*

A one-way/ return-trip ticket to…	**Un billet aller simple/aller-retour…** *uhN bee • yay ah • lay sehN • pluh/ ah • lay • ruh • toor…*
How much?	**Combien ça coûte ?** *kohN • beeyehN sah koot*
Which gate/line?	**Quelle porte/ligne ?** *kehl pohrt/lee • nyuh*
Which platform?	**Quel quai ?** *kehl kay*
Where can I get taxi?	**Où puis-je prendre un taxi ?** *oo pwee • zhuh a prawN • druh uhN tahk • see*
Take me to this address.	**Conduisez-moi à cette adresse.** *kohN • dwee • zay • mwah ah seh tah • drehs*
Can I have a map?	**Puis-je avoir une carte ?** *pwee • zhuh ah • vwahr ewn kahr*

TICKETS

When's…to Paris?	**Quand est…pour Paris ?** *kawN tay…poor pah • ree*
the (first) bus	**le (premier) bus** *luh (pruh • meeyay) bews*
the (next) flight	**le (prochain) vol** *luh (proh • shehN) vohl*
the (last) train	**le (dernier) train** *luh (dehr • neeyay) trehN*
Where do I buy a ticket?	**Où puis-je acheter un billet ?** *oo pwee • zhuh ah • shtay uhN bee • yay*
One/Two ticket(s).	**Un/Deux billet(s).** *uhN/duh bee • yay*

For today/tomorrow.	**Pour aujourd'hui/demain.**
	poor oh • zhoor • dwee/duh • mehN
A…ticket.	**Un billet…**
	uhN bee • yay…
one-way	**aller simple**
	nah • lay sehN • pluh
return trip	**aller-retour**
	nah • lay • ruh • toor
first class	**première classe**
	pruh • meeyehr klahs
business class	**classe affaire**
	klahs ah • fehr
economy class	**classe économique**
	klah say • koh • noh • meek
How much?	**Combien ça coûte ?**
	kohN • beeyehN sah koot
Is there a discount for…?	**Y-a-t-il une réduction pour…?**
	yah • teel ewn ray • dewk • see • yohN poor…
children	**les enfants**
	lay zawN • fawN
students	**les étudiants**
	lay zay • tew • dee • yawN
senior citizens	**les seniors**
	lay say • nyohr
tourists	**les touristes**
	lay too • reehst
The express bus/express train, please.	**Le bus direct/L'express, s'il vous plaît.**
	luh bews dee • rehkt/lehk • sprehs seel voo play
The local bus/train, please.	**Le bus/train régional, s'il vous plaît.**
	luh bews/trehN ray • zheeyoh • nahl seel voo play
I have an e-ticket.	**J'ai un billet électronique.**
	zhay uhN bee • yay ay • lehk • troh • neek

Can I buy a ticket on the bus/train?	**Puis-je acheter un billet dans le bus/ train ?**
	pwee • zhuh ah • shtay uhN bee • yay dawN luh bews/trehN
Do I have to stamp the ticket before boarding?	**Dois-je composter mon billet avant de monter ?**
	dwah • zhuh kohN • poh • stay mohN bee • yay ah • vawN duh mohN • tay
How long is this ticket valid?	**Jusqu'à quand le billet est-il valable ?**
	zhew • skah kawN luh bee • yay eh • teel vah • lah • bluh
Can I return on the same ticket?	**Puis-je utiliser le même billet pour le retour ?**
	pwee • zhuh ew • tee • lee • zay luh mehm bee • yay poor luh rhuh • toor
I'd like to… my reservation.	**Je voudrais…ma réservation.**
	zhuh voo • dray…mah ray • zehr • vah • seeyohN
cancel	**annuler**
	ah • new • lay
change	**échanger**
	ay • shawN • zhay
confirm	**confirmer**
	kohN • feer • may

For Time, see page 23.

AIRPORT TRANSFER

How much is a taxi to the airport?	**Combien coûte le trajet en taxi jusqu'à l'aéroport ?**
	kohN • beeyehN koot luh trah • zhay awN tahk • see zhew • skah lah • ay • roh • pohr
To…Airport, please.	**À l'aéroport de…, s'il vous plaît.**
	ah lah • ay • roh • pohr duh…seel voo play

My flight leaves at…	**Mon vol part à…**
	mohN vohl pahr ah…
I'm in a rush.	**Je suis pressé *m*/pressée *f*.**
	zhuh swee preh • say
My airline is…	**Ma compagnie aérienne est…**
	mah kohN • pah • nee ah • ay • ree • yeh nay…
Can you take an alternate route?	**Pouvez-vous prendre une route différente ?**
	poo • vay • voo prawN • druh ewn root dee • fay • rawNt
Can you drive faster/slower?	**Pouvez-vous conduire plus/moins vite ?**
	poo • vay • voo kohN • dweer plew/mwehN veet

YOU MAY SEE…

LES ARRIVÉES	arrivals
LES DÉPARTS	departures
RETRAIT DES BAGAGES	baggage claim
SÉCURITÉ	security
VOLS NATIONAUX	domestic flights
VOLS INTERNATIONAUX	international flights
ENREGISTREMENT	check-in
ENREGISTREMENT ÉLECTRONIQUE	e-ticket check-in
PORTES DE DÉPART	departure gates

YOU MAY HEAR...

**Quelle compagnie aérienne
prenez-vous ?**
*kehl kohN • pah • nee ah • ay • ree • yehn
pruh • nay • voo*

What airline are
you flying?

Nationale ou internationale ?
*nah • seeyoh • nahl oo
ehN • tehr • nah • seeyoh • nahl*

Domestic or
international?

Quel terminal ?
kehl tehr • mee • nahl

What terminal?

France has more than 20 main airports. The two
main airports in Paris are Roissy-Charles de Gaulle, located
15 miles (23 km) north of the city, and Orly, located 9 miles
(14 km) south of the city. Air France is France's principal
domestic airline, with services between major cities: Paris,
Lille, Lyon, Strasbourg, Grenoble, Bordeaux, Clermont-
Ferrand, Nantes, Marseilles, Nice, Toulouse and more.

CHECKING IN

Where's check-in?	**Où est l'enregistrement ?** *oo ay lawN • ruh • zhees • truh • mawN*
My name is…	**Je m'appelle…** *zhuh mah • pehl…*
I'm going to…	**Je vais à…** *zhuh vay ah…*
I have…	**J'ai…** *zhay…*
one suitcase	**une valise** *ewn vah • leez*
two suitcases	**deux valises** *duh vah • leez*
one piece of hand luggage	**un bagage à main** *uhN bah • gahzh ah mehN*
How much luggage is allowed?	**Combien de bagages sont permis ?** *kohN • beeyehN duh bah • gahzh sohN pehr • mee*
Is that pounds or kilos?	**Est-ce que ce sont des livres ou des kilos ?** *ehs kuh suh sohN day leevr oo day kee • loh*
Which terminal?	**Quel terminal ?** *kehl tehr • mee • nahl*
Which gate?	**Quelle porte ?** *kehl pohrt*
I'd like a window/aisle seat.	**Je voudrais un siège hublot/couloir.** *zhuh an voo • dray uhN see • yehzh ew • bloh/kool • wahr*
When do we leave/arrive?	**Quand est-ce que nous partons/arrivons ?** *kawN tehs kuh noo pahr • tohN/ zah • ree • vohN*

Is the flight delayed?	**Est-ce que le vol est retardé ?**
	ehs kuh luh vohl ay ruh•tahr•day
How late?	**Combien de retard a-t-il ?**
	kohN•beeyehN duh ruh•tahr ah•teel

YOU MAY HEAR...

Au suivant !	Next!
oh swee•vawN	
Votre passeport/billet, s'il vous plaît.	Your passport/
ticket, voh•truh pahs•pohr/bee•yay	please.
seel voo play	
Avez-vous des bagages à enregistrer ?	Are you checking
in ah•vay•voo day bah•gahzh ah	any luggage?
awN•ruh•zhees•tray	
C'est trop gros pour un bagage à main.	That's too large
troh groh poor uhN bah•gahzh ah mehN	for a carry-on
	[piece of hand
	luggage].
Avez-vous fait ces bagages	Did you pack
vous-même ?	these bags
ah•vay•voo feh seh bah•gahzh	yourself?
voo•mehm	
Est-ce que quelqu'un vous a donné	Did anyone give
quelque chose à porter ?	you anything to
ehs kuh kehl•kuhN voo zah doh•nay	carry?
kehl•kuh shoh zah pohr•tay	
Retirer vos chaussures.	Take off your
ruh•tee•ray voh shoh•sewr	shoes.
Embarquement immédiat...	Now boarding...
awN•bahr•kuh•mawN ee•meh•dyah...	

LUGGAGE

Where is/are…?	**Où est/sont…?**
	oo ay/sohN…
the luggage trolleys	**les chariots**
	lay shah•ree•yoh
the luggage lockers	**les consignes**
	lay kohN•see•nyuh
the baggage claim	**le retrait des bagages**
	luh ruh•tray day bah•gahzh
My luggage has been lost/stolen.	**Mon bagage a été perdu/volé.**
	mohN bah•gahzh ah ay•tay pehr•dew/ voh•lay
My suitcase is damaged	**Ma valise est endommagée.**
	mah vah•leez ay awN•doh•mah•zhay

FINDING YOUR WAY

Where is/are…?	**Où est/sont…?**
	oo ay/sohN…
the currency exchange	**le bureau de change**
	luh bew•roh duh shawNzh
the car hire	**l'agence de voitures de location**
	lah•zhawNs duh vwah•tewr duh loh•kah•seeyohN
the exit	**la sortie**
	lah sohr•tee
the taxis	**les taxis**
	lay tahk•see
Is there… into town?	**Est-ce qu'il y a…pour aller en ville ?**
	ehs keel•yah…poor ah•lay awN veel
a bus	**un bus**
	uhN bews

a train	**un train**
	uhN trehN
a metro	**un métro**
	uhN may•troh

TRAIN

Where's the train station?	**Où est la gare ?**
	oo ay lah gahr
How far is it?	**C'est loin d'ici ?**
	say lwehN dee•see
Where is/are…?	**Où est/sont…?**
	oo ay/sohN…
the ticket office	**le bureau de vente des billets**
	luh bew•roh duh vawNt day bee•yay
the information desk	**le bureau de renseignements**
	luh bew•roh duh rawN•seh•nyuh•mawN
the luggage lockers	**les consignes**
	lay kohN•see•nyuh
the platforms	**les quais**
	lay kay
Can I have a schedule [timetable]?	**Puis-je avoir les horaires ?**
	pwee•zhuh ah•vwahr lay zhoh•rehr

How long is the trip?	**Combien de temps dure le voyage ?**
	kohN • beeyehN duh tawN dewr luh
	vwah • yahzh
Is it a direct train?	**Est-ce que c'est un train direct ?**
	ehs kuh say tuhN trehN dee • rehkt
Do I have to	**Est-ce que je dois changer de train ?**
change trains?	*ehs kuh zhuh dwah shawN • zhay duh trehN*
Is the train on time?	**Est-ce que le train est à l'heure ?**
	ehs kuh luh trehN ay aht luhr

For Tickets, see page 45.

France has a fast and efficient train network
operated by **SNCF** (**Société Nationale des
Chemins de Fer**). The **SNCF** links over 50 cities in France,
with the central hub in Paris. Paris has six train stations
that service the rest of France and Europe. The **TGV** (**Train
à Grande Vitesse**) is an extra-high-speed train that runs
routes from Paris to Bordeaux, Brest, La Rochelle, Lille,
Calais, Lyon and Marseille. Advance reservations are usually
required.
The **Eurostar** offers fast and frequent service from London
(St Pancras, or Ebbsfleet and Ashford in Kent) to Paris. The
Eurotunnel provides car travel from Folkestone, U.K., to
Calais, France.

YOU MAY SEE...

QUAIS	platforms
INFORMATION	information
RÉSERVATIONS	reservations
SALLE D'ATTENTE	waiting room
ARRIVÉES	arrivals
DÉPARTS	departures

DEPARTURES

Which track [platform] to...?	**Quel quai pour...?** *kehl kay poor...*
Is this the track [platform]/ train to...?	**Est-ce que c'est le quai/train pour...?** *ehs kuh say luh kay/trehN poor...*
Where is track	**Où est le quai...?** *oo ay luh kay... [platform]...?*
Where do I change for...?	**Où dois-je changer pour...?** *oo dwah • zhuh shawN • zhay poor...*

YOU MAY HEAR...

Billets, s'il vous plaît. *bee • yay seel voo play*	Tickets, please.
Vous devez changer à... *voo duh • vay shawN • zhay ah...*	You have to change at...
Prochain arrêt... *proh • shehN nah • reh...*	Next stop...

ON BOARD

Can I sit here/open the window?	**Puis-je m'asseoir ici/ouvrir la fenêtre ?**
	pwee • zhuh mah • swahr ee • see/ oo • vreer lah fuh • neh • truh
That's my seat.	**C'est ma place.**
	say mah plahs
Here's my reservation.	**Voici ma réservation.**
	vwah • see mah ray • sehr • vah • seeyohN

BUS

Where's the bus station?	**Où est la gare routière ?**
	oo ay lah gahr roo-tee-yehr
How far is it?	**C'est loin d'ici ?**
	say lwehN dee • see
How do I get to…?	**Comment vais-je à…?**
	koh • mawN vay • zhuh ah…
Is this the bus to…?	**Est-ce le bus pour…?**
	ehs luh bews poor…
Can you tell me when to get off?	**Pouvez-vous me dire quand je dois descendre ?**
	poo • vay • voo muh deer kawN zhuh dwah deh • sawN • druh
Do I have to change buses?	**Est-ce que je dois changer de bus ?**
	ehs kuh zhuh dwah shawN • zhay duh bews
Stop here, please!	**Arrêtez-vous ici, s'il vous plaît !**
	ah • ray • tay • voo ee • see seel voo play

For Asking Directions, see page 64.

Bus tickets can be purchased from the bus driver, or you can buy them in metro stations or at tobacconists. Tickets purchased for the metro can also be used for the bus system. Remember to validate your ticket in the machine when boarding the bus.

YOU MAY SEE...

ARRÊT DE BUS	bus stop
DEMANDER L'ARRÊT	request stop
ENTRÉE/SORTIE	entrance/exit
COMPOSTER VOTRE BILLET	stamp your ticket

METRO

Where's the metro station?
Où est la station de métro ?
oo ay lah stah • seeyohN duh may • troh

A map, please.
Une carte, s'il vous plaît.
ewn kahrt seel voo play

Which line for...?
Quelle est la ligne pour...?
keh lay lah lee • nyuh poor...

Which direction?
Quelle direction ?
kehl dee • rayk • seeyohN

Do I have to transfer [change]?
Est-ce que je dois changer de ligne ?
ehs kuh zhuh dwah shawN • zhay duh lee • nyuh

Is this the metro to...?
Est-ce que c'est le métro pour...?
ehs kuh say luh may • troh poor...

How many stops to...?	**Combien d'arrêts jusqu'à...?**
	kohN • beeyehN dah • ray zhew • skah...
Where are we?	**Où sommes-nous ?**
	oo suhm • noo

For Tickets, see page 45.

Many of France's major cities have metro [subway] systems, including Paris, Lille, Toulouse, Lyon, Marseille, Rennes and Rouen.

The metro systems are well marked with easy-to-read maps available at the stations. Most systems run from approximately 5:00 a.m. until 12:00 a.m., with some running slightly shorter or longer hours. In most cities, the same tickets work for the bus, metro and tram systems. Some cities require a ticket for each leg of the journey, while others allow you to travel the entire network on one ticket. Tickets can usually be purchased at the station or at tobacconists and other retailers.

BOAT & FERRY

When is the ferry to...?	**Quand part le ferry pour...?**
	kawN pahr luh fay • ree poor...
Can I take my car?	**Est-ce que je peux prendre ma voiture ?**
	ehs kuh zhuh puh prawN • druh mah vwah • tewr
What time is the next sailing?	**À quelle heure est le prochain bateau ?**
	ah kehl luhr ay luh proh • shehN bah • toh
Can I book a seat/ cabin?	**Puis-je réserver un siège/une cabine ?**
	pwee • zhuh ray • zehr • vay uhN see • yehzh/ewn kah • been

How long is the crossing?	**Combien de temps dure la traversée ?** *kohN • beeyehN duh tawN dewr lah trah • vehr • say*

For Weather, see page 41.

YOU MAY SEE...

CANOTS DE SAUVETAGE	life boats
GILET DE SAUVETAGE	life jacket

Ferry services operate to and from the U.K., the Republic of Ireland and the Channel Islands to the north of France. Ferries carry cars as well as passengers. Services can be booked through the individual ferry companies or through a travel agent.

TAXI

Where can I get a taxi?	**Où puis-je prendre un taxi ?** *oo pwee • zhuh prawN • druh uhN tahk • see*
Can you send a taxi?	**Pouvez-vous envoyer un taxi ?** *poo • vay • voo awN • vwah • yay uhN tahk • see*
Do you have the number for a taxi?	**Avez-vous le numéro d'un taxi ?** *ah • vay • voo number for a taxi? luh new • may • roh duhN tahk • see*

I'd like a taxi now/ for tomorrow at…	**Je voudrais un taxi maintenant/pour demain à…**
	zhuh voo • dray uhN tahk • see mehN • tuh • nawN/poor duh • mehN ah…
Pick me up at…	**Prenez-moi à…**
	pruh • nay • mwah ah…
I'm going to…	**Je vais à…**
	zhuh vay zah…
this address	**cette adresse**
	seh tah • drehs
the airport	**l'aéroport**
	lah • ay • roh • pohr
the train station	**la gare**
	lah gahr
I'm late.	**Je suis en retard.**
	zhuh swee zawN ruh • tahr
Can you drive faster/slower?	**Pouvez-vous conduire plus/moins vite ?**
	poo • vay • voo kohN • dweer plew/mwehN veet
Stop/Wait here.	**Arrêtez/Attendez ici.**
	ah • ray • tay/ah • tawN • day ee • see
How much?	**Combien ça fait ?**
	kohN • beeyehN sah fay

You said it would cost…

Vous aviez dit que cela coûterait…
voo zah • veeyay dee kuh suh • lah koo • tuh • ray…

Keep the change.

Gardez la monnaie.
gahr • day lah moh • nay

YOU MAY HEAR…

Pour où ?
poor oo

Where to?

Quelle est l'adresse ?
keh lay lah • drehs

What's the address?

Il y a une surcharge le soir/pour l'aéroport.
eel • yah ewn sewr • shahrzh luh swahr/poor lah • ay • roh • pohr

There's a nighttime/airport surcharge.

A taxi can be hailed on the street; available taxis can be spotted by the lit sign on the roof of the car. You can also wait for a taxi at stands, commonly located near train stations, metro stations and other tourist spots. Though tipping the driver isn't the norm, it's nice to do so for good service. There is usually a surcharge for each piece of luggage. The rate per kilometer may be different at night and for trips to the airport.

BICYCLE & MOTORBIKE

I'd like to hire…	**Je voudrais louer…**
	zhuh voo • dray looway…
a bicycle	**une bicyclette**
	ewn bee • see • kleht
a moped	**une mobylette**
	ewn moh • bee • leht
a motorcycle	**une moto**
	ewn moh • toh
How much per day/week?	**Combien par jour/semaine?**
	kohN • beeyehN pahr zhoor/suh • mehn
Can I have a helmet/lock?	**Puis-je avoir un casque/cadenas?**
	pwee • zhuh ah • vwahr uhN kas • kuh/ kah • duh • nah

CAR HIRE

Where's the car hire?	**Où est l'agence de location de voitures?**
	oo ay lah • zhawNs duh loh • kah • seeyohN duh vwah • tewr
I'd like…	**Je voudrais…**
	zhuh voo • dray…
a cheap/small car	**une voiture bon marché/petite voiture**
	ewn vwah • tewr bohN mahr • shay/ puh • teet vwah • tewr
an automatic/ a manual	**une automatique/manuelle**
	ewn oh • toh • mah • teek/mah • new • ehl
air conditioning	**la climatisation**
	lah klee • mah • tee • zah • seeyohN
a car seat	**un siège bébé**
	uhN seeyehzh bay • bay

How much…?	**Combien ça coûte…?**
	kohN • beeeyehN sah koot…
per day/week	**par jour/semaine**
	pahr zhoor/suh • mehN
per kilometer	**par kilomètre**
	pahr kee • loh • meh • truh
for unlimited mileage	**pour un kilométrage illimité**
	poor uhN kee • loh • meh • trahzh ee • lee • mee • tay
with insurance	**avec assurance**
	ah • vehk ah • sew • rawNs
Are there any discounts?	**Y-a-t-il des réductions ?**
	yah • teel day ray • dewk • seeyohN

For Numbers, see page 20.

YOU MAY HEAR…

Avez-vous un permis de conduire international ?	Do you have an international driver's license?
ah • vay • voo uhN pehr • mee duh kohN • dweer ehN • tehr • nah • seeyoh • nahl	
Votre passeport, s'il vous plaît.	Your passport, please.
voh • truh pahs • pohr seel voo play	
Voulez-vous prendre une assurance ?	Do you want insurance?
Voo • lay • voo prawN • druh ewn ah • sew • rawNs	
J'ai besoin d'un acompte.	I'll need a deposit.
zhay buh • zwehN duhN ah • kohNt	
Vos initiales/Signez ici.	Initial/Sign here.
voh zee • nee • seeyahl/see • nyay zee • see	

FUEL STATION

Where's the fuel station?	**Où est la station service ?**
	oo ay lah stah • seeyohN sehr • vees
Fill it up.	**Faites-le plein.**
	feht • luh plehN
…euros, please.	**…euros, s'il vous plaît.**
	…uh • roh seel voo play
I'll pay in cash/by credit card.	**Je paierai en espèces/par carte de crédit.**
	zhuh pay • ray awN nehs • pehs/pahr kahrt duh kray • dee

For Numbers, see page 20.

YOU MAY SEE…

ESSENCE	gas [petrol]
SANS PLOMB	unleaded
ORDINAIRE	regular
SUPER	super
GAZOLE	diesel

ASKING DIRECTIONS

Is this the way to…?	**Est-ce le chemin pour…?**
	ehs luh shuh • mehN poor…
How far is it to…?	**À quelle distance se trouve…?**
	ah kehl dees • tawNs suh troov…
Where's…?	**Où est…?**
	oo ay…
…Street	**la rue…**
	lah rew…

this address	**cette adresse**
	seh tah • drehs
the highway [motorway]	**l'autoroute**
	loh • toh • root
Can you show me on the map?	**Pouvez-vous me montrer sur la carte ?**
	poo • vay • voo muh mohN • tray sewr lah kahrt
I'm lost.	**Je suis perdu** *m*/**perdue** *f*.
	zhuh swee pehr • dew

YOU MAY SEE...

 STOP — stop

 CÉDEZ LE PASSAGE — yield

 STATIONNEMENT INTERDIT — no parking

 SENS UNIQUE — one way

 SENS INTERDIT — no entry

 CIRCULATION INTERDITE — no vehicles allowed

 INTERDICTION DE DÉPASSER — no passing

 FEU TRICOLORE — traffic signal ahead

SORTIE — exit

YOU MAY HEAR...

tout droit *too drwah*	straight ahead
à gauche *ah gohsh*	left
à droite *ah drwaht*	right
au coin *oh kwehN*	around the corner
à l'opposé *ah loh • poh • zay*	opposite
derrière *deh • reeyehr*	behind
près de *pray duh*	next to
après *ah • pray*	after
nord/sud *nohr/sewd*	north/south
est/ouest *ehst/oowehst*	east/west
au feu (tricolore) *oh fuh (tree • koh • lohr)*	at the traffic light
au carrefour *oh cahr-foor*	at the intersection

PARKING

Can I park here?	**Puis-je me garer ici ?** *pwee•zhuh muh gah•ray ee•see*
Where's...?	**Où est...?** *oo ay...*
the parking garage	**le garage** *luh gah•rahzh*
the parking lot [car park]	**le parking** *luh pahr•keeng*
the parking meter	**l'horodateur** *loh•roh•dah•tuhr*
How much...?	**Combien ça coûte...?** *kohN•beeyehN sah koot...*
per hour	**par heure** *pahr uhr*
per day	**par jour** *pahr zhoor*
for overnight	**toute la nuit** *toot lah nwee*

Parking in larger cities is sometimes hard to find. Parking on the street is possible; you'll usually have to purchase a ticket from a machine for a certain length of time and display it in your windshield. Parking is not allowed on red marked areas or near yellow-marked curbs. Parking garages can be found in downtown areas, though their rates can be expensive.

BREAKDOWN & REPAIR

My car broke down/ won't start.	**Ma voiture est tombée en panne/ne démarre pas.** *mah vwah • tewr ay tohN • bay awN pahn/nuh day • mahr pah*
Can you fix it (today)?	**Pouvez-vous la réparer (aujourd'hui) ?** *poo • vay • voo lah ray • pah • ray (oh • zhoor • dwee)*
When will it be ready?	**Quand cela sera-t-il prêt ?** *kawN suh • lah suh • rah • teel pray*
How much?	**Combien ça coûte ?** *kohN • beeyehN sah koot*
I have a puncture/ flat tyre [tire].	**J'ai un pneu crevé/Mon pneu est crevé.** *zhay uhN pnuh kruh • vay/mohN pnuh ay kruh • vay*

For Emergencies, see page 142.

ACCIDENTS

My car broke down/ won't start.	**Ma voiture est tombée en panne/ne démarre pas.** *mah vwah • tewr ay tohN • bay awN pahn/ nuh day • mahr pah*
Can you fix it (today)?	**Pouvez-vous la réparer (aujourd'hui) ?** *poo • vay • voo lah ray • pah • ray (oh • zhoor • dwee)*

For Police, see page 144.

PLACES TO STAY

NEED TO KNOW

Can you recommend a hotel?	**Pouvez-vous me conseiller un hôtel?**
	poo • vay • voo muh kohN • say • yay uhN noh • tehl
I made a reservation.	**J'ai fait une réservation.**
	zhay fay ewn ray • zehr • vah seeyohN
My name is…	**Mon nom est…**
	mohN nohN ay…
Do you have a room…?	**Avez-vous une chambre…?**
	ah • vay • voo ewn shawN • bruh…
for one/two	**pour un/deux**
	poor uhN/duh
with a bathroom	**avec salle de bains**
	ah • vehk sahl duh behN
with air conditioning	**avec climatisation**
	ah • vehk klee • mah • tee • zah • seeyohN
For…	**Pour…**
	poor…
tonight	**ce soir**
	suh swahr
two nights	**deux nuits**
	duh nwee
one week	**une semaine**
	ewn suh • mehn
How much?	**Combien ça coûte ?**
	kohN • beeyehN sah koot

Is there anything cheaper?	**N'y-a-t-il rien de moins cher ?**
	Nee • yah • teel reeyehN duh mwehN shehr
When's check-out?	**Quand dois-je quitter la chambre ?**
	kawN dwah • zhuh kee • tay lah shawN • bruh
Can I leave this in the safe?	**Puis-je laisser ceci dans le coffre ?**
	pwee • zhuh lay • say suh • see dawN luh koh • fruh
Can I leave my bags?	**Puis-je laisser mes bagages ?**
	pwee • zhuh lay • say meh bah • gahzh
Can I have my bill/ a receipt?	**Puis-je avoir ma facture/un reçu ?**
	pwee • zhuh ah • vwahr mah fahk • tewr/uhN ruh • sew
I'll pay in cash/by credit card.	**Je paierai en espèces/par carte de crédit.**
	zhuh pay • ray awN nehs • pehs/pahr kahrt duh kray • dee

SOMEWHERE TO STAY

Can you recommend...?	**Pouvez-vous me conseiller...?**
	poo • vay • voo muh kohN • say • yay...
a hotel	**un hôtel**
	uhN noh • tehl
a hostel	**une auberge de jeunesse**
	ewn oh • behrzh duh zhuh • nehs
a campsite	**un camping**
	uhN kawN • peeng
a bed and breakfast	**un bed and breakfast**
	uhN behd ahnd brayk • fahst

What is it near?	**C'est près de quoi ?**
	say pray duh kwah
How do I get there?	**Comment est-ce que je m'y rends ?**
	koh • mawN ehs kuh zhuh mee rawN

For Asking Directions, see page 64.

AT THE HOTEL

If you didn't reserve accommodations before your trip, visit the local **Office de Tourisme** (Tourist Information Office) for recommendations on places to stay.

Hotels in France are ranked in categories or stars; the higher the category or number of stars, the more luxurious and expensive the hotel. **Relais** and **châteaux** are former castles, monasteries, manor houses or abbeys that have been converted into high-end accommodations. **Gîtes-chambres d'hôte** are rentable guestrooms, usually in a village home or on a farm, sometimes referred to as agritourism. Condos, apartments and villas are available for those with larger groups or families or who are staying in one place for at least a week. Hostels and campsites are also available.

I have a reservation.	**J'ai une réservation.**
	zhay ewn ray • zehr • vah • seeyohN
My name is…	**Mon nom est…**
	mohN nohN may…

Do you have a room...?	**Avez-vous une chambre...?**
	ah • vay • voo ewn shawN • bruh...
with a toilet/shower	**avec toilettes/douche**
	ah • vehk twah • leht/doosh
with air conditioning	**climatisée**
	klee • mah • tee • zay
that's smoking/ non-smoking	**fumeur/non-fumeur**
	few • muhr/ nohN • few • muhr
For...	**Pour...**
	poor...
tonight	**ce soir**
	suh swahr
two nights	**deux nuits**
	duh nwee
a week	**une semaine**
	ewn suh • mehn
Do you have...?	**Avez-vous...?**
	ah • vay • voo...
a computer	**un ordinateur**
	uhN nohr • dee • nah • tuhr
an elevator [a lift]	**un ascenseur**
	uhN nah • sawN • suhr
(wireless) internet service	**une connexion internet (Wi-Fi)**
	ewn koh • nek • seeyohN ehN • tehr • neht (wee • fee)
room service	**un service de chambres**
	uhN sehr • vees duh shawN • bruh
a pool	**une piscine**
	ewn pee • seen
a gym	**une salle de gym**
	ewn sahl duh zheem
I need...	**J'ai besoin...**
	zhay buh • zwehN...
an extra bed	**d'un lit supplémentaire**
	duhN lee sew • play • mawN • tehr

a cot	**d'un lit pliant**
	duhN lee plee • yawN
a crib	**d'un berceau**
	duhN behr • soh

For Online, see page 86.

YOU MAY HEAR…

Votre passeport/carte de crédit, s'il vous plaît.
voh • truh pahs • pohr/kahrt duh kray • dee seel voo play

Your passport/ credit card, please.

Remplissez cette fiche.
rawN • plee • say seht feesh

Fill out this form.

Signez ici.
see • nyay ee • see

Sign here.

PRICE

How much per night/week?	**Quel est le tarif par nuit/semaine ?**
	kehl eh luh tah-reef pahr nwee/suh • mehn
Does that include breakfast/tax?	**Est-ce que cela comprend le petit déjeuner/la TVA ?**
	ehs kuh suh • lah kohN • prawN luh puh • tee day • zhuh • nay/lah tay • vay • ah
Are there any discounts?	**Y-a-t-il des réductions ?**
	yah • teel deh ray • dewk • seeyohN

For Numbers, see page 20.

PREFERENCES

Can I see the room?	**Puis-je voir la chambre ?**
	pwee • zhuh vwahr lah shawN • bruh
I'd like a...room.	**Je voudrais une chambre...**
	zhuh voo • dray ewn shawN • bruh...
better	**plus confortable**
	plew kohN • fohr • tah • bluh
bigger	**plus grande**
	plew grawNd
cheaper	**moins chère**
	mwehN shehr
quieter	**plus calme**
	plew kahlm
I'll take it.	**Je la prends.**
	zhuh lah prawN
No, I won't take it.	**Non, je ne la prends pas.**
	nohN zhuh nuh lah prawN pah

QUESTIONS

Where is/are...?	**Où est/sont...?**
	oo ay/sohN...
the bar	**le bar**
	luh bahr
the bathrooms	**les toilettes**
	lay twah • leht
the elevator [lift]	**l'ascenseur**
	lah • sawN • suhr
I'd like...	**Je voudrais...**
	zhuh voo • dray...
a blanket	**une couverture**
	ewn koo • vehr • tewr

an iron	**un fer à repasser**
	uhN feh rah ruh • pah • say
the room key/key card	**la clé/carte de la chambre**
	lah klay/kahrt duh lah shawN • bruh
a pillow	**un oreiller**
	uhN noh • reh • yay
soap	**du savon**
	dew sah • vohN
toilet paper	**du papier toilette**
	dew pah • pee • yay twah • leht
a towel	**une serviette**
	ewn sehr • veeyeht
Do you have an adapter for this?	**Avez-vous un adaptateur pour ceci ?**
	ah • vay • voo uhN nah • dahp • tah • tuhr poor suh • see
How do you turn on the lights?	**Comment allume-t-on les lumières ?**
	koh • mawN ah • lewm • tohN lay lew • mee • yehr
Can you wake me at…?	**Pouvez-vous me réveiller à…?**
	poo • vay • voo muh ray • veh • yay ah…
Can I leave this in the safe?	**Puis-je laisser ceci dans le coffre ?**
	pwee • zhuh lay • say suh • see dawN luh koh • fruh
Can I have my things from the safe?	**Puis-je prendre mes affaires qui sont dans le coffre ?**
	pwee • zhuh prawN • druh meh zah • fehr kee sohN dawN luh koh • fruh
Is there mail/ a message for me?	**Y-a-t-il du courrier/un message pour moi ?**
	yah • teel dew koo • reeyay/uhN meh • sahzh poor mwah
Do you have a laundry service?	**Avez-vous un service de blanchisserie ?**
	ah • vay • voo uhN sehr • vees duh blawN • shee • suh • ree

YOU MAY SEE...

POUSSER/TIRER	push/pull
TOILETTES	bathroom [toilet]
DOUCHES	showers
ASCENSEUR	elevator [lift]
ESCALIERS	stairs
DISTRIBUTEURS	vending machines
GLACE	ice
TEINTURERIE	laundry
NE PAS DÉRANGER	do not disturb
PORTE COUPE-FEU	fire door
SORTIE (DE SECOURS)	(emergency) exit
APPEL RÉVEIL	wake-up call

PROBLEMS

There's a problem.	**Il y a un problème.** *eel • yah uhN proh • blehm*
I lost my key/ key card.	**J'ai perdu la clé/carte de ma chambre.** *zhay pehr • dew lah klay/kahrt duh mah shawN • bruh*
I've locked my key/key card in the room.	**J'ai laissé ma clé/carte à l'intérieur de ma chambre.** *zhay leh • say mah klay/kahrt ah lehN • tay • reeyuhr duh mah shawN • bruh*
There's no hot water/toilet paper.	**Il n'y a pas d'eau chaude/de papier toilette.** *eel nee • yah pah doh shohd/duh pah • pee • yay twah • leht*
The room is dirty.	**La chambre est sale.** *lah shawN • bruh ay sahl*

There are bugs in the room.	**Il y a des insectes dans la chambre.** *eel • yah day zehN • sehkt dawN lah shawN • bruh*
…doesn't work.	**…ne fonctionne pas.** *…nuh fohNk • seeyohn pah*
Can you fix…?	**Pouvez-vous réparer…?** *poo • vay • voo ray • pah • ray…*
the air conditioning	**la climatisation** *lah klee • mah • tee • zah • seeyohN*
the fan	**le ventilateur** *luh vawN • tee • lah • tuhr*
the heat [heating]	**le chauffage** *luh shoh • fahzh*
the light	**la lumière** *lah lew • mee • yehr*
the TV	**la télé** *lah tay • lay*
the toilet	**les toilettes** *lay twah • leht*
I'd like another room.	**Je voudrais une autre chambre.** *zhuh voo • dray zewn oh • truh shawN • bruh*

Unlike the U.S., most of Europe runs on 220-volt electricity, and plugs are two-pronged. You may need a converter and/or an adapter for your appliance.

CHECKING OUT

When's check-out?	**Quand dois-je quitter la chambre ?** *kawN dwah • zhuh kee • tay lah shawN • bruh*

Can I leave my bags here until…?	**Puis-je laisser mes bagages ici jusqu'à…?**
	pwee•zhuh leh•say meh bah•gahzh ee•see zhew•skah…
Can I have an itemized bill/ a receipt?	**Puis-je avoir une facture détaillée/un reçu?**
	pwee•zhuh ah•vwahr ewn fahk•tewr day•tie•yay/uhN ruh•sew
I think there's a mistake.	**Je pense qu'il y a une erreur.**
	zhuh pawNs keel•yah ewn ay•ruhr
I'll pay in cash/by credit card.	**Je paierai en espèces/par carte de crédit.**
	zhuh pay•ray awN nehs/pehs/pahr kahrt duh kray•dee

At hotels, it is common to leave tips for services provided. If you are happy with the housekeeping service, leave a tip of € 1–2 per day for the housekeeper in your room when you leave. Tip porters and your concierge € 2–3 if they provide assistance.

RENTING

I reserved an apartment/a room.	**J'ai réservé un appartement/une chambre.**
	zhay ray•zehr•vay uhN nah•pahrt•mawN/ewn shawN•bruh
My name is…	**Je m'appelle…**
	zhuh mah•pehl…
Can I have the keys?	**Puis-je avoir les clés ?**
	pwee•zhuh ah•vwahr lay klay

Are there…?	**Y-a-t-il des…?**
	yah • teel day…
dishes	**assiettes**
	ah • seeyeht
pillows	**oreillers**
	oh • reh • yay
sheets	**draps**
	drah
towels	**serviettes**
	sehr • veeyeht
kitchen utensils	**ustensiles de cuisine**
	ews • tawN • seel duh kwee • zeen
When do I put out the bins/	**Quand dois-je sortir les poubelles/ ordures à recycler?**
	kawN dwah • zhuh sohr • teer lay recycling? poo • behl/zohr • dewr ah ruh • seek • lay
…is broken.	**…est cassé m /cassée f.**
	…ay kah • say
How does… work?	*Comment fonctionne…?*
	koh • mawN fohNk • seeyohn…
the air conditioner	**la climatisation**
	lah klee • mah • tee • zah • seeyohN
the dishwasher	**le lave-vaisselle**
	luh lahv • veh • sehl

the freezer	**le congélateur**	
	luh kohN•zhay•lah•tuhr	
the heater	**le chauffage**	
	luh shoh•fahzh	
the microwave	**le micro-onde**	
	luh mee•kroh•ohNd	
the refrigerator	**le réfrigérateur**	
	luh ray•free•zhay•rah•tuhr	
the stove	**la gazinière**	
	lah gah•zee•neeyehr	
the washing machine	**la machine à laver**	
	lah mah•sheen ah lah•vay	

For the Dictionary, see page 234.

DOMESTIC ITEMS

I need...	**J'ai besoin...**	
	zhay buh•zwehN...	
an adapter	**d'un adaptateur**	
	duhN nah•dahp•tah•tuhr	
aluminum [foil]	**de papier aluminium**	
	duh pah•peeyay ah•lew•mee•neeyewm	
a bottle opener	**d'un ouvre-bouteille**	
	duhN oo•vruh•boo•tehy	
a broom	**d'un balai**	
	duhN bah•lay	
a can opener	**d'un ouvre boîte**	
	duhN noo•vruh bwaht	
cleaning supplies	**de produits d'entretien**	
	duh proh•dwee dawN•truh•teeyehN	
a corkscrew	**d'un tire-bouchon**	
	duhN teer•boo•shohN	
detergent	**de détergent**	
	duh day•tehr•zhawN	

dishwashing liquid	**de détergent pour lave-vaisselle**	
	duh day • tehr • zhawN poor lahv • veh • sehl	
bin bags	**de sacs poubelles**	
	duh sahk poo • behl	
a lightbulb	**d'une ampoule**	
	dewn nawN • pool	
matches	**d'allumettes**	
	dah • lew • meht	
a mop	**d'une serpillière**	
	dewn sehr • peeyehr	
napkins	**de serviettes de table**	
	duh sehr • veeyeht duh tah • bluh	
paper towels	**de serviettes en papier**	
	duh sehr • veeyeht awN pah • peeyay	
plastic wrap [cling film]	**de cellophane**	
	duh seh • loh • fahn	
a plunger	**d'un déboucheur de toilettes**	
	duhN day • boo • shur duh twah • leht	
scissors	**de ciseaux**	
	duh see • zoh	
a vacuum cleaner	**d'un aspirateur**	
	duhN nah • spee • rah • tuhr	

For In the Kitchen, see page 195.

AT THE HOSTEL

Is there a bed available?	**Y-a-t-il un lit de libre ?**	
	yah • teel uhN lee duh lee • bruh	
I'd like…	**Je voudrais…**	
	zhuh voo • dray…	
a single/double room	*une chambre simple/double*	
	ewn shawN • bruh sehN • pluh/doo • bluh	
a blanket	**une couverture**	
	ewn koo • vehr • tewr	

a pillow	**un oreiller**
	uhN noh•reh•yay
sheets	**des draps**
	day drah
a towel	**une serviette de bain**
	ewn sehr•veeyeht duh behN
Do you have lockers?	**Avez-vous des cadenas ?**
	ah•vay•voo day cah•duh•nah
When do you up?	**Quand fermez-vous ?**
	kawN fehr•may•voo lock
Do I need a membership card?	**Ai-je besoin d'une carte de membre ?**
	ay•zhuh buh•zwehN dewn kahrt duh mawN•bruh
Here's my international student card.	**Voici ma carte internationale d'étudiant.**
	vwah•see mah kahrt ehN•tehr•nah•seeyoh•nahl day•tew•deeyawN

ⓘ

You will need to show your accredited Youth Hostel Association card to stay in a French hostel run by the **Fédération Unie des Auberges de Jeunesse (FUAJ)** or the **Ligue Française pour les Auberges de Jeunesse (LFAJ)**. **Gîtes d'Étapes** offer hostel accommodation that is popular with hikers, usually in or near national parks where no membership is needed.
Hostels fill up quickly during tourist seasons; make reservations well in advance. Many hostels accept online reservations too.

GOING CAMPING

Can I camp here?	**Puis-je camper ici ?**
	pwee • zhuh kawN • pay ee • see
Where's the campsite?	**Où est le camping ?**
	oo ay luh kawN • peeng
What is the charge per day/week?	**Quel est le prix par jour/semaine ?**
	keh lay luh pree pahr zhoor/suh • mehn
Are there...?	**Y-a-t-il...?**
	yah • teel...
cooking facilities	**des cuisines**
	day kwee • zeen
electric outlets	**des prises électriques**
	day pree zay • lehk • treek
laundry facilities	**des buanderies**
	day bew • awN • dree
showers	**des douches**
	day doosh
tents for hire	**des tentes à louer**
	day tawN tah looway
Where can I empty the chemical toilet?	**Où puis-je vider les toilettes portables ?**
	oo pwee • zhuh vee • day lay twah • leht pohr • tah • bluh

For Domestic Items, see page 80.

YOU MAY SEE...

EAU POTABLE	drinking water
CAMPING INTERDIT	no camping
FEUX DE BOIS/BARBECUES INTERDITS	no fires/ barbecues

COMMUNICATIONS

NEED TO KNOW

Where's an internet cafe?	**Où y-a-t-il un cyber café ?** *oo yah • teel uhN see • behr kah • fay*
Can I access the internet/check my e-mail?	**Puis-je me connecter à Internet/ consulter mes mails ?** *pwee • zhuh muh koh • nehk • tay ah ehN • tehr • neht/kohN • sewl • tay may mehyl*
How much per half hour/hour?	**Combien coûte la demi-heure/ l'heure ?** *kohN • beeyehN koot lah duh • mee • uhr/ luhr*
How do I connect/log on?	**Comment est-ce que je me connecte/j'ouvre une session ?** *koh • mawN ehs kuh zhuh muh koh • nehkt/zhoo • vruh ewn seh • seeyohN*

A phone card, please.	**Une carte de téléphone, s'il vous plaît.**
	ewn kahrt duh tay • lay • fohn seel voo play
Can I have your phone number?	**Puis-je avoir votre numéro de téléphone ?**
	pwee • zhuh ah • vwahr voh • truh new • meh • roh duh tay • lay • fohn
Here's my number/e-mail.	**Voici mon numéro/mail.**
	vwah • see mohN new • meh • roh/mehyl
Call me.	**Appelle-moi.**
	ah • pehl • mwah
E-mail me.	**Envoie-moi un mail.**
	awN • vwah • mwah uhN mehyl
Hello. This is…	**Bonjour. C'est…**
	bohN • zhoor say…
Can I speak to…?	**Puis-je parler à…?**
	pwee • zhuh pahr • lay ah…
Can you repeat that?	**Pouvez-vous répéter cela ?**
	poo • vay • voo ray • pay • tay suh • lah
I'll call back later.	**Je rappellerai plus tard.**
	zhuh rah • peh • luh • ray plew tahr
Bye.	**Au revoir.**
	oh ruh • vwahr
Where's the post office?	**Où est la poste ?**
	oo ay lah pohst
I'd like to send this to…	**Je voudrais envoyer ceci à…**
	zhuh voo • dray zawN • vwah • yay suh • see ah…

French language purists prefer to avoid using words adopted directly from English, but their best efforts can't always change popular usage. Even though you may see and hear the official dictionary-approved word for e-mail, **courriel** (short for **courrier-électronique**, electronic mail), the word **mail** is the one most often used in France and what you will see used throughout this book.

ONLINE

Where's an internet cafe?	**Où y-a-t-il un cyber café ?**
	oo yah • teel uhN see • behr kah • fay
Does it have wireless internet?	**Est-ce qu'il a la connexion Wi-Fi ?**
	ehs kee • lee ah lah koh • nehk • seeyohN wee • fee
What is the WiFi password?	**Quel est le mot de passe du WiFi ?**
	keh lay luh moh duh pahs dew wee • fee
Is the WiFi free?	**Est-ce que le WiFi est gratuit ?**
	ehs kuh luh wee • fee ay grah • twee
Do you have bluetooth?	**Avez-vous Bluetooth ?**
	ah • vay • voo bloo • toohs

Can you show me how to turn on/off the computer?	**Pouvez-vous me montrer comment allumer/éteindre l'ordinateur ?** *poo • vay • voo muh mohN • tray koh • mawN ah • lew • may/ eh • tehyuhn • druh lohr • dee • nah • tuhr*
Can I…?	**Puis-je…?** *pwee • zhuh…*
access the internet	**accéder à Internet** *ahk • seh • day ah ehN • tehrneht*
check my email	**consulter mes mails** *kohN • sewl • tay may mehyl*
print	**imprimer** *ehN • pree • may*
plug in/charge my laptop/iPhone/iPad/BlackBerry?	**brancher/charger mon ordinateur portable/iPhone/iPad/Blackberry ?** *brawN • shay/shahr • zhay mohN nohr • dee • nah • tuhr pohr • tah • bluh/ ee • fohn/ee • pahd/black • ber • ee*
access Skype?	**accéder à Skype ?** *ah • ksay • day ah skiep*
How much per half hour/hour?	**Combien coûte la demi-heure/l'heure ?** *kohN • beeyehN koot lah duh • mee • uhr/ luhr*
How do I…?	**Comment est-ce que…?** *koh • mawN ehs kuh…*
connect/disconnect	**je me connecte/déconnecte** *zhuh muh koh • nehkt/day • koh • nehkt*
log on/off	**j'ouvre/je termine la session** *zhoo • vruh/zhuh tehr • meen lah seh • seeyohN*
type this symbol	**je frappe ce symbole** *zhuh frahp suh sehN • bohl*
What's your email?	**Quel est votre mail ?** *keh lay voh • truh mehyl*

My email is…   **Mon mail est…**
                mohN mehyl ay…

Do you have   **Avez-vous un scanneur ?**
a scanner?   *ah • vay • voo uhN skah • nuhr*

SOCIAL MEDIA

Are you on   **Etes-vous sur Facebook/Twitter ?** *(polite*
Facebook/Twitter?   *form)*
                    eht • voo sewr fayhs • book/twee • teuhr
                    Es-tu sur Facebook/Twitter ? *(informal*
                    form)
                    eh • tew sewr fayhs • book/twee • teuhr

What's your user   **Quel est votre nom d'utilisateur ?** *(polite*
name?   *form)*
                    keh lay voh • truh nohN
                    dew • tee • lee • zah • tuhr
                    Quel est ton nom d'utilisateur? *(informal*
                    form)
                    keh lay tohN nohN
                    dew • tee • lee • zah • tuhr

I'll add you as a   **Je vous ajouterai comme ami.** *(polite*
friend.   *form)*
                    zhuh voo zah • zhoo • tray kohm ah • mee
                    Je t'ajouterai comme ami. *(informal form)*
                    zhuh tah • zhoo • tray kohm ah • mee

I'll follow you on **Je vous suivrai sur Twitter.** *(polite form)*
Twitter.   *zhuh voo swee • vray sewr twitter*
                    Je te suivrai sur Twitter. *(informal form)*
                    zhuh tuh swee • vray sewr twitter

Are you following…? **Suivez-vous…?** *(polite form)*
                    swee • vay voo
                    Suis-tu…? *(informal form)*
                    swee tew

I'll put the pictures on Facebook/Twitter. **Je mettrai les photos sur Facebook/Twitter.**

zhuh may • tray lay foh • toh sewr fayhs • book/twee • teuhr

I'll tag you in the pictures. **Je vous marquerai sur les photos.** *(polite form)*

zhuh voo mahr • kuh • ray sewr lay foh • toh

Je te marquerai sur les photos. *(informal form)*

zhuh tuh mahr • kuh • ray sewr lay foh • toh

YOU MAY SEE...

FERMER	close
SUPPRIMER	delete
MAIL	e-mail
SORTIR	exit
AIDE	help
MESSAGERIE INSTANTANÉE	instant messenger
INTERNET	internet
OUVRIR UNE SESSION	log in
NOUVEAU (MESSAGE)	new (message)
ALLUMÉ/ÉTEINT	on/off
OUVRIR	open
IMPRIMER	print
SAUVEGARDER	save
ENVOYER	send
NOM UTILISATEUR/MOT DE PASSE	username/ password
CONNEXION WI-FI	wireless internet

PHONE

A phone card/ prepaid phone, please.	**Une carte de téléphone/téléphone prépayé, s'il vous plaît.** *ewn kahrt duh tay•lay•fohn/ tay•lay•fohn pray•pay•yay seel voo play*
How much?	**Combien ça coûte ?** *kohN•beeyehN sah koot*
Where's the pay phone?	**Où y-a-t-il une cabine téléphonique ?** *oo yah•teel ewn kah•been tay•lay•foh•neek*
What's the area/ country code for…?	**Quel est le code régional/national pour…?** *keh lay luh kohd ray•zheeyoh•nahl/ nah•seeyoh•nahl poor…*
What's the number for Information?	**Quel est le numéro des renseignements ?** *keh lay luh new•may•roh day rawN•seh•nyuh•mawN*
I'd like the number for…	**Puis-je avoir le numéro de…** *pwee•zhuh ah•vwahr luh new•may•roh duh…*

I'd like to call collect [reverse the charges].	**Je voudrais appeler en PCV.** *zhuh voo • dray zah • puh • lay awN pay • say • vay*
My phone doesn't work here.	**Mon téléphone est en panne.** *mohN tay • lay • fohn ayt awN pahn*
What network are you on?	**Quel réseau utilisez-vous ?** *kehl ray • zoh ew • tee • lee • zay voo*
Is it 3G?	**Est-ce que c'est un réseau 3G ?** *ehs kuh say uhN ray • zoh trwah zhay*
I have run out of credit/minutes.	**J'ai épuisé mon crédit/mes minutes.** *zhay ay • pwee • zay mohN kray • dee/meh mee • newt*
Can I buy some credit?	**Puis-je acheter du crédit ?** *pwee • zhuh ah • shtay dew kray • dee*
Do you have a phone charger?	**Avez-vous un chargeur pour téléphone ?** *ah • vay • voo uhN shahr • zhuhr poor tay • lay • fohn*
Can I have your number?	**Puis-je avoir votre numéro ?** *pwee • zhuh ah • vwahr voh • truh new • meh • roh*
Here's my number.	**Voici mon numéro.** *vwah • see mohN new • may • roh*
Please call/text me.	**S'il vous plaît, appelez-moi/ envoyez-moi un SMS.** *seel voo play ah • puh • lay • mwah/ awN • vwah • yay • mwah uhN ehs • ehm • ehs*
I'll call/text you.	**Je vous appellerai/enverrai un SMS.** *zhuh voo zah • peh • luh • ray/ zawN • veh • ray uhN nehs • ehm • ehs*

For Numbers, see page 20.

TELEPHONE ETIQUETTE

Hello. This is…	**Bonjour. C'est…** *bohN • zhoor say…*
Can I speak to…?	**Puis-je parler à…?** *pwee • zhuh pahr • lay ah…*
Extension…	**Poste…** *pohst…*
Speak louder/more slowly, please.	**Parlez plus fort/lentement, s'il vous plaît.** *pahr • lay plew fohr/lawN • tuh • mawN seel voo play*
Can you repeat that?	**Pouvez-vous répéter cela ?** *poo • vay • voo ray • pay • tay suh • lah*
I'll call back later.	**Je rappellerai plus tard.** *zhuh rah • peh • luh • ray plew tahr*
Bye.	**Au revoir.** *oh ruh • vwahr*

Most pay phones in France are card operated; some require phone cards, others, credit cards. You can purchase phone cards at **tabacs** (tobacconists), at **la Poste** (the post office) and wherever you see the sign **Télécarte**. French phone numbers have 10 digits, including a two digit regional prefix. When calling within the country, you must dial all 10 digits, even when dialing within the same region. When dialing from outside the country, delete the first 0 (part of the regional prefix).

To call the U.S. or Canada from France, dial 001 + area code + phone number. To call the U.K. from France, dial 0044 + area code (minus the first 0) + phone number.

YOU MAY HEAR...

Qui est à l'appareil ?
kee ay aht lah • pah • rehy

Who's calling?

Attendez un instant.
ah • tawN • day uhN nehN • stawN

Hold on.

Je vous le *m*/la *f* passe.
zhuh voo luh /lah pahs

I'll put you through to him/her.

Il *m*/Elle *f* n'est pas là/est sur une autre ligne.
Eel /ehl nay pah lah/ay sewr ewn oh • truh lee • nyuh

He/She is not here/on another line.

Voulez-vous laisser un message ?
voo • lay • voo leh • say uhN meh • sahzh

Would you like to leave a message?

Rappelez plus tard/dans dix minutes.
rah • puh • lay plew tahr/dawN dee mee • newt

Call back later/in ten minutes.

Peut-il *m*/Peut-elle *f* vous rappeler ?
puh • teel /puh • tehl voo rah • puh • lay

Can he/she call you back?

Quel est votre numéro de téléphone ?
keh lay voh • truh new • may • roh duh tay • lay • fohn

What's your number?

FAX

Can I send/receive a fax here?	**Puis-je envoyer/recevoir un fax ici ?** *pwee • zhuh awN • vwah • yay/ ruh • suh • vwah ruhN fahks ee • see*
What's the fax number?	**Quel est le numéro de fax ?** *keh lay luh new • may • roh duh fahks*
Please fax this to…	**S'il vous plaît, faxer ceci au…** *seel voo play fahk • say suh • see oh…*

POST

Where's the post office/mailbox?	**Où est la poste/boîte aux lettres ?** *oo ay lah pohst/bwah • toh • leh • truh*
A stamp for this postcard/letter to…	**Un timbre pour cette carte postale/ lettre pour…** *uhN tehN • bruh poor seht kahrt pohs • tahl/leh • truh poor…*
How much?	**Combien ça coûte ?** *kohN • beeyehN sah koot*
Send this package by airmail/express.	**Envoyez ce paquet par avion/en express.** *awN • vwah • yay suh pah • keh pah rah • veeyohN/awN ehk • sprehs*

A receipt, please.   **Un reçu, s'il vous plaît.**
uhN ruh • sew seel voo play

YOU MAY HEAR...

Remplissez ce formulaire de   Fill out the
déclaration de douane.   customs
rawN • plee • say suh fohr • mew • lehr duh   declaration form.
day • klah • rah • seeyohN duh doo • wahn

Quelle est la valeur ?   What's the
keh lay lah vah • luhr   value?

Qu'est-ce qu'il y a à l'intérieur ? What's inside?
kehs keel • yah ah lehN • tay • reeyuhr

Most branches of **la Poste** (the post office) are open
from 8:00 a.m. to 7:00 or 8:00 p.m., Monday through Friday.
On Saturdays, most post offices close at noon. In addition to
standard postal services, you will also be able to do banking
here and ATMs can be found at many locations.

SIGHTSEEING

NEED TO KNOW

Where's the tourist information office?	**Où est l'office de tourisme?** *oo ay loh • fees duh too • ree • smuh*
What are the main sights?	**Quelles sont les choses importantes à voir?** *kehl sohN lay shoh zehN • pohr • tawN tah vwahr*
Do you offer tours in English?	**Proposez-vous des visites en anglais?** *Proh • poh • zay • voo day vee • zeet awN nawN • glay*
Can I have a map/guide?	**Puis-je avoir une carte/un guide?** *pwee • zhuh ah • vwahr ewn kahrt/uhN geed*

TOURIST INFORMATION

Do you have information on...?	**Avez-vous des renseignements sur...?** *ah • vay • voo day rawN • seh • nyuh • mawN sewr...*
Can you recommend...?	**Pouvez-vous me conseiller...?** *poo • vay • voo muh kohN • say • yay...*

a bus tour	**une visite en bus**
	ewn vee • zeet awN bews
an excursion to…	**une excursion pour…**
	ewn ehk • skewr • seeyohN poor…
a sightseeing tour of…	**une visite de…**
	ewn vee • zeet duh…

Offices de tourisme or syndicats d'initiative
(tourism offices) are usually located near the downtown area,
next to train stations or close to city hall. They can provide
a wealth of information about lodging, entertainment,
restaurants, etc.

ON TOUR

I'd like to go on the excursion to…	**Je voudrais faire cette excursion à…**
	zhuh voo • dray fehr seh
	tehk • skewr • seeyohN nah…
When's the next tour?	**Quand a lieu la prochaine visite ?**
	kawN tah leeyuh lah proh • shehn vee • zeet
Are there tours in English?	**Y-a-t-il des visites en anglais ?**
	yah • teel day vee • zeet zawN nawN • glay
Is there an English guide book/audio guide?	**Y-a-t-il un guide/audio guide en anglais ?**
	yah • teel uhN geed/oh • deeyoh geed
	awN nawN • glay
What time do we leave/return?	**À quelle heure partons-nous/revenons-nous ?**
	ah keh luhr pahr • tohN • noo/
	ruh • vuh • nohN-noo
We'd like to see…	**Nous voudrions voir…**
	noo voo • dreeyohN vwahr…

Can we stop here…?	**Pouvons-nous nous arrêter ici pour…?**
	poo • vohN • noo noo zah • reh • tay ee • see poor…
to take photos	**prendre des photos**
	prawN • druh day foh • toh
for souvenirs	**acheter des souvenirs**
	ah • shtay day soo • vuh • neer
for the toilets	**aller aux toilettes**
	ah • lay oh twah • leht
Is it disabled-accessible?	**Est-ce que c'est accessible aux handicapés ?**
	ehs kuh say tahk • say • see • bluh oh zawN • dee • kah • pay

For Tickets, see page 20.

SEEING THE SIGHTS

Where's…?	**Où est…?**
	oo ay…
the battleground	**le champ de bataille**
	luh shawN duh bah • tie
the botanical garden	**le jardin botanique**
	luh zhahr • dehN boh • tah • neek
the castle	**le château**
	luh shah • toh
the downtown area	**le centre-ville**
	luh sawN • truh • veel
the fountain	**la fontaine**
	lah fohN • tehn
the library	**la bibliothèque**
	lah bee • bleeyoh • tehk
the market	**le marché**
	luh mahr • shay

the museum	**le musée**
	luh mew•zay
the old town	**la vieille ville**
	lah veeyeh•yuh veel
the opera house	**l'opéra**
	loh•pay•rah
the palace	**le palais**
	luh pah•lay
the park	**le parc**
	luh pahrk
the ruins	**les ruines**
	lay rween
the shopping area	**le quartier commercial**
	luh kahr•teeyay koh•mehr•seeyahl
the town square	**la grand-place**
	lah grawN-plahs
Can you show me on the map?	**Pouvez-vous me montrer sur la carte ?**
	poo•vay-voo muh mohN•tray sewr lah kahrt
It's…	**C'est…**
	say…
amazing	**surprenant**
	sewr•preh•nawN

beautiful	**beau**
	boh
boring	**ennuyeux**
	awN • nwee • yuh
interesting	**intéressant**
	ehN • tay • reh • sawN
magnificent	**magnifique**
	mah • nee • feek
romantic	**romantique**
	roh • mawN • teek
strange	**étrange**
	ay • trawNzh
terrible	**terrible**
	teh • ree • bluh
ugly	**laid**
	lay
I (don't) like it.	**Je (n')aime (pas).**
	zhuh (n)ehm (pah)

For Asking Directions, see page 64.

RELIGIOUS SITES

Where's...?	**Où est...?**
	oo ay...
the cathedral	**la cathédrale**
	lah kah • tay • drahl
the Catholic/	**l'église catholique/protestante**
Protestant church	*lay • gleez kah • toh • leek/*
	proh • tehs • tawNt
the mosque	**la mosquée**
	lah mohs • kay
the shrine	**le lieu saint**
	luh leeyuh sehN
the synagogue	**la synagogue**
	lah see • nah • gohg
the temple	**le temple**
	luh tawN • pluh
What time is the service?	**À quelle heure est la messe ?**
	ah keh luhr ay lah mehs

LEISURE TIME

SHOPPING 104

SPORT & LEISURE 126

TRAVELING WITH CHILDREN 136

SHOPPING

NEED TO KNOW

Where's the market/mall?	**Où est le marché/centre commercial ?**
	oo ay luh mahr • shay/sawN • truh koh • mehr • seeyahl
I'm just looking.	**Je regarde seulement.**
	zhuh ruh • gahrd suhl • mawN
Can you help me?	**Pouvez-vous m'aider ?**
	poo • vay • voo meh • day
I'm being helped.	**On s'occupe de moi.**
	ohN soh • kewp duh mwah
How much?	**Combien ça coûte ?**
	kohN • beeyehN sah koot
That one, please.	**Celui-ci** *m***/Celle-ci** *f***, s'il vous plaît.**
	suh • lwee • see/sehl see seel voo play
That's all.	**C'est tout.**
	say too
Where can I pay?	**Où puis-je payer ?**
	oo pwee • zhuh pay • yay
I'll pay in cash/by credit card.	**Je paierai en espèces/par carte de crédit.**
	zhuh pay • ray awN neh • spehs/pahr kahrt duh kray • dee
A receipt, please.	**Un reçu, s'il vous plaît.**
	uhN ruh • sew seel voo play

AT THE SHOPS

Where's...?	**Où est...?**
	oo ay...
the antiques store	**l'antiquaire**
	lawN • tee • kehr
the bakery	**la boulangerie**
	lah boo • lawN • zhuh • ree
the bank	**la banque**
	lah bawNk
the bookstore	**la librairie**
	lah lee • breh • ree
the clothing store	**le magasin de vêtements**
	luh mah • gah • zehN duh veht • mawN
the delicatessen	**la charcuterie**
	lah shar • kew • tuh • ree
the department store	**le grand magasin**
	luh grawN mah • gah • zehN store
the gift shop	**la boutique cadeaux**
	lah boo • teek kah • doh
the health food store	**le magasin de diététique**
	luh mah • gah • zehN duh deeyay • tay • teek
the jeweler	**la bijouterie**
	lah bee • zhoo • tuh • ree
the liquor store [off-licence]	**le marchand de vins et de spiritueux**
	luh mahr • shawN duh vehN ay duh spee • ree • tewuh
the market	**le marché**
	luh mahr • shay
the music store	**le disquaire**
	luh dees • kehr
the pastry shop	**la pâtisserie**
	lah pah • tee • suh • ree

the pharmacy	**la pharmacie**
	lah fahr • mah • see
the produce [grocery] store	**le magasin de fruits et légumes**
	luh mah • gah • zehN duh frwee zay lay • gewm
the shoe store	**le magasin de chaussures**
	luh mah • gah • zehN duh shoh • sewr
the shopping mall	**le centre commercial**
	luh sawN • truh koh • mehr • seeyahl
the souvenir store	**le magasin de souvenirs**
	luh mah • gah • zehN duh soo • vuh • neer
the supermarket	**le supermarché**
	luh sew • pehr • mahr • shay
the tobacconist	**le bureau de tabac**
	luh bew • roh duh tah • bahk
the toy store	**le magasin de jouets**
	luh mah • gah • zehN duh zhooway

For Souvenirs, see page 123.

ASK AN ASSISTANT

When do you open/close?	**À quelle heure ouvrez-vous/ fermez-vous ?**
	ah kehl uhr oo • vray • voo/fehr • may • voo
Where's...?	**Où est...?**
	oo ay...
the cashier	**la caisse**
	lah kehs
the escalator	**l'escalator**
	lehs • kah • lah • tohr
the elevator [lift]	**l'ascenseur**
	lah • sawN • suhr
the fitting room	**la cabine d'essayage**
	lah kah • been deh • say • yahzh

the store directory	**le plan du magasin**
	luh plawN dewmah • gah • zehN
Can you help me?	**Pouvez-vous m'aider ?**
	poo • vay • voo meh • day
I'm just looking.	**Je regarde seulement.**
	zhuh ruh • gahrd suhl • mawN
I'm being helped.	**On s'occupe de moi.**
	ohN soh • kewp duh mwah
Do you have…?	**Avez-vous…?**
	ah • vay • voo…
Can you show me…?	**Pouvez-vous me montrer…?**
	poo • vay • voo muh mohN • tray…
Can you ship/ wrap it?	**Pouvez-vous le livrer/l'emballer ?**
	poo • vay • voo luh lee • vray/lawN • bah • lay
How much?	**Combien ça coûte ?**
	kohN • beeyehN sah koot
That's all.	**C'est tout.**
	say too

For Clothing, see page 114.

YOU MAY HEAR…

Je peux vous aider ?
zhuh puh voo zeh • day

Can I help you?

Un instant.
uhN nehNs • tawN

One moment.

Que désirez-vous ?
kuh day • zee • ray-voo

What would you like?

Autre chose ?
oh • truh shohz

Anything else?

YOU MAY SEE...

OUVERT/FERMÉ	**open**/closed
FERMÉ POUR LE DÉJEUNER	closed for lunch
CABINE D'ESSAYAGE	fitting room
CAISSE	cashier
ESPÈCES SEULEMENT	cash only
CARTES ACCEPTÉES	credit cards accepted
HEURES D'OUVERTURE	business hours
SORTIE	exit

PERSONAL PREFERENCES

I'd like something…	**Je voudrais quelque chose…**
	zhuh voo • dray kehl • kuh shohz…
cheap/expensive	**de bon marché/cher**
	duh bohN mahr • shay/shehr
larger/smaller	**de plus grand/petit**
	duh plew grawN/puh • tee
from this region	**de cette région**
	duh seht ray • zheeyohN
Around…euros.	**Pour à peu près…euros.**
	poor ah puh pray…uh • roh
Is it real?	**Est-ce que c'est du vrai ?**
	ehs kuh say dew vray
Can you show me this/that?	**Pouvez-vous me montrer ceci/cela ?**
	poo • vay-voo muh mohN • tray suh • see/ suh • lah
That's not quite what I want.	**Ce n'est pas exactement ce que je veux.**
	suh nay pah zehk • sahk • tuh • mawN suh kuh zhuh vuh

No, I don't like it.	**Non, je n'aime pas.**
	nohN zhuh nehm pah
It's too expensive.	**C'est trop cher.**
	say troh shehr
I have to think about it.	**Je dois réfléchir.**
	zhuh dwah ray • flay • sheer
I'll take it.	**Je le m/la f prends.**
	zhuh luh /lah prawN

PAYING & BARGAINING

How much?	**Combien ça fait ?**
	kohN • beeyehN sah fay
I'll pay…	**Je paierai…**
	zhuh pay • ray…
in cash	**en espèces**
	awN nehs • pehs
by credit card	**par carte de crédit**
	pahr kahrt duh kray • dee
by traveler's cheque	**avec des chèques de voyages**
	ah • vehk day shehk duh vwah • yahzh
A receipt, please.	**Un reçu, s'il vous plaît.**
	uhN ruh • sew seel voo play
That's too much.	**C'est beaucoup trop.**
	say boh • koo troh
I'll give you…	**Je vous en propose…**
	zhuh voo zawN proh • pohz…
I have only…euros.	**Je n'ai que…euros.**
	zhuh nay kuh…uh • roh
Is that your best price?	**Est-ce que c'est votre meilleur prix ?**
	ehs kuh say voh • truh mehy • yuhr pree
Can you give me a discount?	**Pouvez-vous me faire une remise ?**
	poo • vay-voo muh fehr ewn ruh • meez

For Numbers, see page 20.

Cash (the euro) is always accepted. Credit and debit cards can be used in cash machines and for purchases. Check with your bank before leaving to obtain a PIN for both debit and credit cards; you'll usually be asked to enter your PIN instead of signing when making purchases. Traveler's checks are also widely accepted in France.

YOU MAY HEAR...

Comment voulez-vous payer ?
koh • mawN voo • lay • voo pay • yay
How are you paying?

Votre carte de crédit est refusée.
voh • truh kahrt duh kray • dee tay ruh • few • zay
Your credit card has been declined.

Une pièce d'identité, s'il vous plaît.
ewn peeyehs dee • dawN • tee • tay seel voo play
ID, please.

Nous n'acceptons pas les cartes de crédit.
noo nahk • sehp • tohN pah lay kahrt duh kray • dee
We don't accept credit cards.

En espèces seulement, s'il vous plaît.
awN nehs • pehs suhl • mawN seel voo play
Cash only, please.

MAKING A COMPLAINT

I'd like... **Je voudrais...**
zhuh voo • dray...

to exchange this **échanger ceci**
ay • shawN • zhay suh • see

a refund	**un remboursement**
	uhN rawN • boor • suh • mawN
to see the manager	**voir le responsable**
	vwahr luh rehs • pohN • sah • bluh

SERVICES

Can you recommend...?	**Pouvez-vous me conseiller...?**
	poo • vay • voo muh kohN • say • yay...
a barber	**un coiffeur pour hommes**
	uhN kwah • fuhr poor ohm
a dry cleaner	**une teinturerie**
	ewn tehN • tewr • ree
a laundromat [launderette]	**une laverie automatique**
	ewn lah • vuh • reeoh • toh • mah • teek
a nail salon	**une onglerie**
	ewn ohN • gluh • ree
a spa	**une station de balnéothérapie**
	ewn stah • seeyohN duh bahl • nayoh • tay • rah • pee
a travel agency	**une agence de voyage**
	ewn ah • zhawNs duh vwah • yahzh
Can you...this?	**Pouvez-vous...ceci ?**
	poo • vay • voo...suh • see
alter	**changer**
	shawN • zhay
clean	**nettoyer**
	neh • twah • yay
fix	**raccourcir**
	rah • koor • seer
press	**repasser**
	ruh • pah • say
When will it be ready?	**Quand cela sera-t-il prêt ?**
	kawN suh • lah seh • rah • teel preh

HAIR & BEAUTY

I'd like…	**Je voudrais…**
	zhuh voo • dray…
an appointment for today/ tomorrow	**un rendez-vous pour aujourd'hui/ demain**
	uhN rawN • day • voo poor oh • zhoor • dwee/duh • mehN
some color/ highlights	**une couleur/des mèches**
	ewn koo • luhr/day mehsh
my hair styled/	**une mise en forme/un brushing**
	ewn mee zawN fohrm/uhN bruh • sheeng
a haircut	**une coupe**
	koop
an eyebrow/ bikini wax	**une épilation à la cire des sourcils/du maillot**
	ewn ay • pee • lah • seeyohN nah lah seer day soor • seel/dew mieyoh
a facial	**un soin du visage**
	uhN swehN dew vee • zahzh
a manicure/	**une manucure/pédicure**
	ewn pedicure mah • new • kewr/ pay • dee • kewr

a (sports) massage	**un massage (sportif)**
	uhN mah•sahzh (spohr•teef)
A trim, please.	**Égalisez les pointes, s'il vous plaît.**
	ay•gah•lee•zay lay pwehNt seel voo play
Not too short.	**Pas trop court.**
	pah troh koor
Shorter here.	**Plus court ici.**
	plew koor ee•see
Do you offer…?	**Proposez-vous…?**
	proh•poh•zay•voo…
acupuncture	**de l'acupuncture**
	duh lah•kew•pohNk•tewr
aromatherapy	**de l'aromathérapie**
	duh lah•roh•mah•tay•rah•pee
oxygen treatment	**des soins à l'oxygène**
	day swehN ahlohk•see•zhehn
a sauna	**un sauna**
	uhN soh•nah

Les stations de balnéothérapie (spas) are popular in France; day spas, especially, can be found in Paris and along the French Riviera. Many villages and resorts specialize in water therapies. The hot springs at Dax have been popular since Roman times, and the town is still one of France's most popular spa destinations. Some spas in the Bordeaux region specialize in wine-based therapies. In addition to the therapies, spa towns may also offer beautiful scenery, casinos, restaurants and outdoor activities.

ANTIQUES

How old is it?	**De quand date-t-il** *m* **/date-elle** *f* **?** *duh kawN dah • teel/dah • tehl*
Do you have anything from the...period?	**Avez-vous quelque chose de la période...?** *ah • vay • voo kehl • kuh shohz duh lah pay • reeyohd...*
Do I have to fill out any forms?	**Dois-je remplir des formulaires ?** *dwah • zhuh rawN • pleer day fohr • mew • lehr*
Is there a certificate of authenticity?	**Y-a-t-il un certificat d'authenticité ?** *yah • teel uhN sehr • tee • fee • kah doh • tawN • tee • see • tay*
Can you ship/ wrap it?	**Pouvez-vous le livrer/l'emballer ?** *poo • vay • voo luh lee • vray/lawN • bah • lay*

CLOTHING

I'd like...	**Je voudrais...** *zhuh voo • dray...*
Can I try this on?	**Puis-je essayer ceci ?** *pwee • zhuh eh • say • yay suh • see*

It doesn't fit.	**Ça ne va pas.**
	sah nuh vah pah
It's too…	**C'est trop…**
	say troh…
big/small	**grand/petit**
	grawN/puh • tee
short/long	**court/long**
	koor/lohng
tight/loose	**serré/large**
	seh • ray/lahrzh
Do you have this in size…?	**Avez-vous ceci en taille…?**
	ah • vay • voo suh • see awN tie…
Do you have this in a bigger/smaller size?	**Avez-vous ceci en plus grand/petit ?**
	ah • vay • voo suh • see awN plew grawN/ puh • tee

For Colors, see page 116.

YOU MAY SEE…

HOMMES	men's
FEMMES	women's
ENFANTS	children's

YOU MAY HEAR…

Ça vous va très bien.	That looks great
sah voo vah tray beeyehN	on you.
Comment ça me va ?	How does it fit?
koh • mawN sah muh vah	
Nous n'avons pas votre taille.	We don't have
noo nah • vohN pah voh • truh tie	your size.

Haute couture (designer fashion) and **prêt-à-porter** (ready-to-wear) boutiques can be found throughout Paris. The latest fashions by Dior®, Givenchy®, Saint-Laurent®, Chanel®, Jean-Paul Gaultier®, Ungaro®, Feraud®, Yamamoto® and Hermès® can be found in Paris well before making it to the U.S. or the U.K. Airport boutiques offer tax-free shopping and may have cheaper prices but fewer selections.

COLORS

I'd like something…	**Je voudrais quelque chose de…**
	zhuh voo • dray kehl • kuh shohz duh…
beige	**beige**
	behzh
black	**noir**
	nwahr
blue	**bleu**
	bluh
brown	**marron**
	mah • rohN
green	**vert**
	vehr
gray	**gris**
	gree
orange	**orange**
	oh • rawNzh
pink	**rose**
	rohz
purple	**violet**
	veeyoh • lay

red	**rouge**
	roozh
white	**blanc**
	blawN
yellow	**jaune**
	zhohn

CLOTHES & ACCESSORIES

a backpack	**un sac à dos**
	uhN sahk ah doh
a belt	**une ceinture**
	ewn sehN • tewr
a bikini	**un bikini**
	uhN bee • kee • nee
a blouse	**un chemisier**
	uhN shuh • mee • zeeyay
a bra	**un soutien-gorge**
	uhN soo • teeyehN • gohrzh
briefs [underpants]/ panties	**des slips/des culottes**
	day sleep/day kew • loht
a coat	**un manteau**
	uhN mawN • toh
a dress	**une robe**
	ewn rohb
a hat	**un chapeau**
	uhN shah • poh
a jacket	**une veste**
	ewn vehst
jeans	**un jean**
	uhN zheen
pajamas	**un pyjama**
	uhN pee • zhah • mah
pants [trousers]	**un pantalon**
	uhN pawN • tah • lohN

pantyhose [tights]	**un collant**
	uhN koh • lawN
a purse [handbag]	**un sac à main**
	uhN sahk ah mehN
a raincoat	**un imperméable**
	uhN nehN • pehr • may • ah • bluh
a scarf	**une écharpe**
	ewn ay • sharp
a shirt	**une chemise**
	ewn shuh • meez
shorts	**un short**
	unN shohrt
a skirt	**une jupe**
	ewn zhewp
socks	**des chaussettes**
	day shoh • seht
a suit	**un costume**
	uhN kohs • tewm
sunglasses	**des lunettes**
	day lew • neht
a sweater	**un pull**
	uhN pewl
a sweatshirt	**un sweat-shirt**
	uhN sweht • shuhrt
a swimsuit	**un maillot de bain**
	uhN mie • yoh duh behN
a T-shirt	**un t-shirt**
	uhN tee • shuhrt
a tie	**une cravate**
	ewn krah • vaht
underwear	**un sous-vêtement**
	uhN soo • veht • mawN

FABRIC

I'd like…	**Je voudrais…** *zhuh voo • dray…*
cotton	**du coton** *dew koh • tohN*
denim	**du jean** *dew zheen*
lace	**de la dentelle** *duh lah dawN • tehl*
leather	**du cuir** *dew kweer*
linen	**du lin** *dew lehN*
silk	**de la soie** *duh lah swah*
wool	**de la laine** *duh lah lehn*
Is it machine washable?	**Est-ce lavable en machine ?** *ehs lah • vah • bluh awN mah • sheen*

SHOES

I'd like…	**Je voudrais…**
	zhuh voo • dray…
high-heels/flats	**des talons hauts/plats**
	day tah • lohN oh/plah
boots	**des bottes**
	day boht
loafers	**des mocassins**
	day moh • kah • sehN
sandals	**des sandales**
	day sawN • dahl
shoes	**des chaussures**
	day shoh • sewr
slippers	**des chaussons**
	day shoh • sohN
sneakers	**des tennis**
	day tay • nees
Size…	**Taille…**
	tie…

For Numbers, see page 20.

SIZES

small (S)	**petit**
	puh • tee
medium (M)	**moyen**
	mwah • yawN
large (L)	**grand**
	grawN
extra large (XL)	**très grand**
	tray grawN

petite	**menue**
	muh • new
plus size	**grande taille**
	grawNd tie

NEWSSTAND & TOBACCONIST

Do you sell English-language newspapers?	**Vendez-vous des journaux en anglais ?**
	vawN • day • voo day zhoor • noh awN nawN • glay
I'd like…	**Je voudrais…**
	zhuh voo • dray…
candy [sweets]	**des bonbons**
	day bohN • bohN
chewing gum	**du chewing gum**
	dew shew • weeng guhm
a chocolate bar	**une barre de chocolat**
	ewn bahr duh shoh • koh • lah
a cigar	**un cigare**
	uhN see • gahr
a pack/carton of cigarettes	**un pack/une cartouche de cigarettes**
	uhN pahk/ewn kahr • toosh duh see • gah • reht
a lighter	**un briquet**
	uhN bree • kay
a magazine	**un magazine**
	uhN mah • gah • zeen

You can find many English-language newspapers at newsstands in major cities, at airports and bus and train stations.

matches	**des allumettes**
	day zah • lew • meht
a newspaper	**un journal**
	uhN zhoor • nahl
a pen	**un stylo**
	uhN stee • loh
a postcard	**une carte postale**
	ewn kahrt pohs • tahl
a road/town map of...	**une carte routière/de la ville de...**
	ewn kahrt roo • teeyehr/duh lah veel duh...
stamps	**des timbres**
	day tehN • bruh

PHOTOGRAPHY

I'd like...camera.	**Je voudrais un appareil photo...**
	zhuh voo • dray zuhN nah • pah • rehy foh • toh...
an automatic	**automatique**
	oh • toh • mah • teek
a digital	**numérique**
	new • may • reek
a disposable	**jetable**
	zheh • tah • bluh
I'd like...	**Je voudrais...**
	zhuh voo • dray...
a battery	**une pile**
	ewn peel
digital prints	**des photos numériques**
	day foh • toh new • may • reek
a memory card	**une carte mémoire**
	ewn kahrt may • mwahr
Can I print digital photos here?	**Puis-je imprimer des photos numériques ici ?**
	pwee • zhuh ehN • pree • may day foh • toh new • may • reek ee • see

SOUVENIRS

a bottle of wine	**une bouteille de vin**
	ewn boo • tehy duh vehN
a box of chocolates	**une boîte de chocolats**
	ewn bwaht duh shoh • koh • lah
some crystal	**du cristal**
	dew kree • stahl
a doll	**une poupée**
	ewn poo • pay
some jewelry	**des bijoux**
	day bee • zhoo
a key ring	**un porte-clés**
	uhN pohrt • klay
a postcard	**une carte postale**
	ewn kahrt pohs • tahl
some pottery	**des poteries**
	day poh • tuh • ree
a T-shirt	**un t-shirt**
	uhN tee • shuhrt
a toy	**un jouet**
	uhN zhooway
Can I see this/that?	**Puis-je voir ceci/cela ?**
	pwee • zhuh vwahr suh • see/suh • lah

I'd like...	**Je voudrais...**
	zhuh voo • dray...
a battery	**une pile**
	ewn peel
a bracelet	**un bracelet**
	uhN brahs • lay
a brooch	**une broche**
	ewn brohsh
a clock	**une pendule**
	ewn pawN • dewl
earrings	**des boucles d'oreille**
	day boo • kluh doh • rehy
a necklace	**un collier**
	uhN koh • leeyay
a ring	**une bague**
	ewn bahg
a watch	**une montre**
	ewn mohN • truh
I'd like...	**Je voudrais...**
	zhuh voo • dray...
copper	**du cuivre**
	dew kwee • vruh
crystal	**du cristal**
	dew krees • tahl
diamonds	**des diamants**
	day deeyah • mawN
white/yellow gold	**de l'or blanc/jaune**
	duh lohr blawN/zhohn
pearls	**des perles**
	day pehrl
pewter	**de l'étain**
	duh lay • tehN
platinum	**du platine**
	dew plah • teen

sterling silver	**de l'argent fin**
	duh lahr • zhawN fehN
Is this real?	**Est-ce que c'est du vrai ?**
	ehs kuh say dew vray
Can you engrave it?	**Pouvez-vous le graver ?**
	poo • vay • voo luh grah • vay

France offers a wide array of souvenirs for the traveler. Souvenir shops are located throughout larger cities, especially near tourist destinations. Certain regions in France are known for their specialty items that make great souvenirs and gifts: lace from Alençon, crystal from Baccarat, perfume from Grasse, porcelain from Limoges and the latest fashions from Paris. Markets and specialty shops are great places to find these regional specialties.

France is well-known for its classic and cutting-edge jewelry design. Paris and the French Riviera are home to famous jewelry houses such as Boucheron®, Cartier® and VanCleef & Arpels®.

SPORT & LEISURE

NEED TO KNOW

When's the game?	**Quand a lieu le match ?**
	kawN tah leeyuh luh mahtch
Where's…?	**Où est…?**
	oo ay…
the beach	**la plage**
	lah plazh
the park	**le parc**
	luh pahrk
the pool	**la piscine**
	lah pee•seen
Is it safe to swim here?	**Est-ce que c'est sans danger de nager ici ?**
	ehs kuh say sawN dawN•zhay duh nah•zhay ee•see
Can I hire clubs?	**Puis-je louer des clubs ?**
	pwee•zhuh looway day kluhb
How much per hour?	**Combien ça coûte par heure ?**
	kohN•beeyehN sah koot pahr uhr
How far is it to…?	**À quelle distance se trouve…?**
	ah kehl dees•tawNs suh troov…
Show me on the map, please.	**Montrez-moi sur la carte, s'il vous plaît.**
	mohN•tray•mwah sewr lah kahrt seel voo play

WATCHING SPORT

When's…(game/race/tournament)?	**Quand a lieu (le match/la course/le tournoi)…?**
	kawN tah leeyuh (luh mahtch/lah koors/luh toor•nwah)…
the baseball	**de baseball**
	duh bays•bohl
the basketball	**de basketball**
	duh bahs•keht•bohl
the boxing	**de boxe**
	duh bohks
the cricket	**de cricket**
	duh kree•keh
the cycling	**de cycliste**
	duh see•kleest
the golf	**de golf**
	duh gohlf
the soccer [football]	**de football**
	duh foot•bohl
the tennis	**de tennis**
	duh tay•nees
the volleyball	**de volley-ball**
	duh voh•lee•bohl
Who's playing?	**Qui joue ?**
	kee zhoo
Where's the racetrack/stadium?	**Où est la piste/le stade ?**
	oo ay lah peest/luh stahd
Where can I place a bet?	**Où puis-je parier ?**
	oo pwee•zhuh pah•reeyay

For Tickets, see page 45.

Soccer is France's most popular sport. Water sports, such as canoeing, rafting, fishing and sailing, are also popular, not only on the coast, but along scenic lakes and rivers. France is home to the highest peaks in Europe across three mountain ranges: the Alps, the Pyrenees and the Massif Central. Skiing, snowboarding, snowshoeing, hiking and dog sledding are enjoyed there. Other popular sports include cycling, horseback riding, horse racing, golf, paragliding, parachuting and car racing. France is host to many world-renowned sporting events: **Tour de France** bicycle race, **Le Mans** car race and the International Tennis Championships, to name a few.

Casinos can be found in France, especially along the French Riviera. Sports betting is permitted only on horse races.

PLAYING SPORT

Where is/are…?	**Où est/sont…?**
	oo ay/sohN…
the golf course	**le terrain de golf**
	luh teh • rehN duh gohlf
the gym	**le gymnase**
	luh zheem • nahz
the park	**le parc**
	luh pahrk
the tennis courts	**les courts de tennis**
	lay koor duh tay • nees
How much per…	**Combien ça coûte par…?**
	kohN • beeyehN sah koot pahr…
day	**jour**
	zhoor

hour	**heure**	
	uhr	
game	**partie**	
	pahr • tee	
round	**tour**	
	toor	
Can I rent [hire]…?	**Puis-je louer…?**	
	pwee • zhuh looway…	
some clubs	**des clubs**	
	day kluhb	
some equipment	**des équipements**	
	day zay • keep • mawN	
a racket	**une raquette**	
	ewn rah • keht	

AT THE BEACH/POOL

Where's the beach/pool?	**Où est la plage/piscine ?**	
	oo ay lah plahzh/pee • seen	
Is there a…?	**Y-a-t-il…?**	
	yah • teel…	
kiddie pool	**une pataugeoire**	
	ewn pah • toh • zhwahr	

indoor/outdoor pool	**une piscine intérieure/extérieure**
	ewn pee • seen ehN • tay • reeyuhr/ ehks • tay • reeyuhr
lifeguard	**un secouriste**
	uhN suh • koo • reest
Is it safe...?	**Est-ce sans danger...?**
	ehs sawN dawN • zhay...
to swim	**de nager**
	duh nah • zhay
to dive	**de plonger**
	duh plohN • zhay
for children	**pour les enfants**
	poor lay zawN • fawN
I'd like to hire...	**Je voudrais louer...**
	zhuh voo • dray looway...
a deck chair	**une chaise**
	ewn shehz
diving equipment	**un équipement de plongée**
	uhN nay • keep • mawN duh plohN • zhay
a jet ski	**un jet ski**
	uhN zheht skee
a motorboat	**un bateau à moteur**
	uhN bah • toh ah moh • tuhr
a rowboat	**une barque**
	ewn bahrk
snorkeling equipment	**un équipement de plongée**
	uhN ay • keep • mawN duh plohN • zhay
a surfboard	**un surf**
	uhN suhrf
a towel	**une serviette**
	ewn sehr • veeyeht
an umbrella	**un parasol**
	uhN pah • rah • sohl
water skis	**des skis nautiques**
	day skee noh • teek

a windsurfer	**une planche à voile**
	ewn plawNsh ah vwahl
For…hours.	**Pour…heures.**
	poor…uhr

France has many beaches; the country has long coasts on the English Channel, the Atlantic Ocean and the Mediterranean Sea. Some of the most popular resorts include St. Tropez, Monte Carlo, Cannes, Marseilles, Nice and the island of Corsica in the Mediterranean.

Most beaches have lifeguards on duty during the summer but always check the flags for swimming conditions. A green flag indicates that swimming is allowed, an orange flag indicates swimming is allowed but hazardous, a red flag indicates swimming is not allowed and a yellow flag indicates swimming is inadvisable because of pollution.

WINTER SPORTS

A lift pass for a day/five days, please.	**Un forfait d' un jour/de cinq jours, s'il vous plaît.** *uhN fohr • fay duhN zhoor/duh sehNk zhoor seel voo play*
I'd like to hire…	**Je voudrais louer…** *zhuh voo • dray looway…*
boots	**des bottes** *day boht*
a helmet	**un casque** *uhN kahsk*
poles	**des bâtons** *day bah • tohN*
skis	**des skis** *day skee*
a snowboard	**un snowboard** *uhN snoh • bohrd*
snowshoes	**des raquettes** *day rah • keht*
These are too	**Ceux-ci** *m*/**Celles-ci** *f*/**sont trop**

big/small.	**grands** m/**grandes** f/**petits** m/**petites** f.
	suh • see/sehl • see sohN troh grawN/ grawNd/ puh • tee/puh • teet
Are there lessons?	**Y-a-t-il des leçons ?**
	yah • teel day luh • sohN
I'm a beginner.	**Je suis debutant** m/**debutante** f.
	zhuh swee day • bew • tawN/ day • bew • tawNt
I'm experienced.	**J'ai de l'expérience.**
	zhay duh lehk • spay • reeyawNs

YOU MAY SEE...

REMONTÉES	lifts
REMONTE-PENTES	drag lift
TÉLÉPHÉRIQUE	cable car
TÉLÉSIÈGE	chair lift
DÉBUTANT	novice
INTERMÉDIAIRE	intermediate
EXPERT	expert
PISTE FERMÉE	trail [piste] closed

A trail map, please.	**La carte des pistes, s'il vous plaît.**
	lah kahrt day peest seel voo play

OUT IN THE COUNTRY

A map of..., please.	**Une carte..., s'il vous plaît.**
	ewn kahrt...seel voo play
this region	**de cette région**
	duh seht ray • zheeyohN
the walking routes	**des chemins de randonnées**
	day sheh • mehN duh rawN • doh • nay

the bike routes	**des pistes cyclables**
	day peest see • klah • bluh
the trails	**des sentiers**
	day sawN • teeyay
Is it…?	**Est-ce…?**
	ehs…
easy	**facile**
	fah • seel
difficult	**difficile**
	dee • fee • seel
far	**loin**
	lwehN
steep	**escarpé**
	ehs • kahr • pay
How far is it to…?	**À quelle distance se trouve…?**
	ah kehl dees • tawNs suh troov…
I'm lost.	**Je suis perdu** *m* **/perdue** *f.*
	zhuh swee pehr • dew
Where's…?	**Où est…?**
	oo ay…
the bridge	**le pont**
	luh pohN
the cave	**la grotte**
	lah groht

the desert	**le désert**
	luh day • zehr
the farm	**la ferme**
	lah fehrm
the field	**le champ**
	luh shawN
the forest	**la forêt**
	lah foh • reh
the hill	**la colline**
	lah koh • leen
the lake	**le lac**
	luh lahk
the mountain	**la montagne**
	lah mohN • tah • nyuh
the nature preserve	**le parc naturel**
	luh pahrk nah • tew • rehl
the viewpoint	**le point d'observation**
	luh pwehNdohb • sehr • vah • seeyohN
the park	**le parc**
	luh pahrk
the path	**le chemin**
	luh shuh • mehN
the peak	**le sommet**
	luh soh • may
the picnic area	**l'aire de pique-nique**
	lehr duh peek • neek
the pond	**l'étang**
	lay • tawN
the river	**la rivière**
	lah ree • veeyehr
the sea	**la mer**
	lah mehr
the (hot) spring	**la source (d'eau chaude)**
	lah soors (doh shohd)

the stream	**le ruisseau**
	luh rwee • soh
the valley	**la vallée**
	lah vah • lay
the vineyard	**la vigne**
	lah vee • nyuh
the waterfall	**les cascades**
	lay kahs • kahd

NEED TO KNOW

Is there a discount for kids?	**Y-a-t-il une remise pour les enfants ?**
	yah • teel ewn ruh • meez poor lay zawN • fawN
Can you recommend a babysitter?	**Pouvez-vous me recommander une baby-sitter ?**
	poo • vay • voo muh ruh • koh • mawN • day ewn bah • bee- see • tuhr
Do you have a child's seat/highchair?	**Avez-vous un siège enfant/ une chaise haute ?**
	ah • vay • voo zuhN seeyehzh awN • fawN/zewn shehz oht
Where can I change the baby?	**Où puis-je changer le bébé ?**
	oo pwee • zhuh shawN • zhay luh bay • bay

TRAVELING WITH CHILDREN

OUT & ABOUT

Can you recommend something for kids?	**Pouvez-vous me conseiller quelque chose pour les enfants ?**
	poo • vay • voo muh kohN • say • yay kehl • kuh shohz poor lay zawN • fawN
Where's…?	**Où est…?**
	oo ay…
the amusement park	**le parc d'attractions**
	luh pahrk dah • trahk • seeyohN
the arcade	**la salle de jeux**
	lah sahl duh zhuh
the kiddie [paddling] pool	**la pataugeoire**
	lah pah • toh • zhwahr
the park	**le parc**
	luh pahrk
the playground	**l'aire de jeux**
	lehr duh zhuh
the zoo	**le zoo**
	luh zoh
Are kids allowed?	**Est-ce que les enfants sont autorisés ?**
	ehs kuh lay zawN • fawN sohN toh • toh • ree • zay
Is it safe for kids?	**Est-ce que c'est sans danger pour les enfants ?**
	ehs kuh say sawN dawN • zay poor lay zawN • fawN
Is it suitable for…year olds?	**Est-ce que cela convient aux enfants de…ans ?**
	ehs kuh suh • lah kohN • veeyehN oh zawN • fawN duh…awN

YOU MAY HEAR...

Comme il *m/***elle** *f* **est mignon** *m/* **mignonne** *f* **!**	How cute!
kohm eel/ehl aymee • nyohN/mee • nyohn	
Comment s'appelle-t-il *m/***elle** *f* **?**	What's his/her name?
koh • mawN sah • pehl • teel/tehl	
Quel âge a-t-il *m/***a-t-elle** *f* **?**	How old is he/she?
kehl ahzh ah • teel/ah • tehl	

For Numbers, see page 20.

BABY ESSENTIALS

Do you have...?	**Avez-vous...?**
	ah • vay • voo...
a baby bottle	**un biberon**
	uhN bee • buh • rohN
baby food	**des petits pots**
	day puh • tee poh
baby wipes	**des lingettes pour bébé**
	day lehN • zhet poor bay • bay
a car seat	**un siège bébé**
	uhN seeyehzh bay • bay
a children's menu/portion	**un menu/des portions pour enfants**
	uhN muh • new/day pohr • seeyohN poo rawN • fawN
a child's seat/ highchair	**un siège bébé/une chaise haute**
	uhN seeyehzh bay • bay/ewn shehz oht
a crib/cot	**un berceau/lit pliant**
	uhN behr • soh/ lee pleeyawN
diapers [nappies]	**des couches**
	day koosh

formula	**du lait pour bébé** *dew lay poor bay • bay*
a pacifier [dummy]	**une tétine** *ewn tay • teen*
a playpen	**un parc pour enfant** *uhN pahrk poo rawN • fawN*
a stroller [pushchair]	**une poussette** *ewn poo • seht*
Can I breastfeed the baby here?	**Puis-je allaiter le bébé ici ?** *pwee • zhuh ah • leh • tay luh bay • bay ee • see*
Where can I breastfeed/change the baby?	**Où puis-je allaiter/changer le bébé ?** *oo pwee • zhuh ah • leh • tay/shawN • zhay luh bay • bay*

For Dining with Children, see page 172.

BABYSITTING

Can you recommend a babysitter?	**Pouvez-vous me recommander une baby-sitter ?** *poo • vay • voo muh ruh • koh • mawN • day ewn bah • bee • see • tuhr*
How much do you/they charge?	**Quel est votre/leur tarif ?** *kehl ay voh • truh/luhr tah • reef*
I'll be back at…	**Je reviens à…** *zhuh ruh • veeyehN ah…*
If you need to contact me, call…	**Si vous avez besoin de me contacter, appelez…** *see voo sah • vay buh • swehN duh muh kohN • tahk • tay ah • play…*

For Meals & Cooking, see page 175.

SAFE TRAVEL

EMERGENCIES 142

POLICE 144

HEALTH 146

PHARMACY 154

DISABLED
TRAVELERS 160

EMERGENCIES

NEED TO KNOW

Help!	**Au secours !**
	oh suh • koor
Go away!	**Allez-vous en !**
	ah • lay • voo zawN
Stop, thief!	**Arrêtez, au voleur !**
	ah • reh • tay oh voh • luhr
Get a doctor!	**Allez chercher un docteur !**
	ah • lay shehr • shay uhN dohk • tuhr
Fire!	**Au feu !**
	oh fuh
I'm lost.	**Je suis perdu** *m* **/perdue** *f*.
	zhuh swee pehr • dew
Can you help me?	**Pouvez-vous m'aider ?**
	poo • vay • voo may • day

YOU MAY HEAR...

Remplissez ce formulaire.
rawN • plee • say suh fohr • mew • lehr

Fill out this form.

Vos papiers d'identité, s'il vous plaît.
*voh pah • peeyay dee • dawN • tee • tay
seel voo play*

Your ID, please.

Quand/Où cela s'est-il produit ?
kawN/oo suh • lah say • teel proh • dwee

When/Where did
it happen?

**À quoi ressemble-t-il m/
ressemble-t-elle f ?**
*ah kwah ruh • sawN • bluh • teel/
ruh • sawN • bluh • tehl*

What does he/
she look like?

In an emergency, dial: **17** for the police
18 for the fire brigade
15 for the ambulance

POLICE

NEED TO KNOW

Call the police!
Appelez la police !
ah • puh • lay lah poh • lees

Where's the
police station?
Où est le commissariat de police ?
*oo ay luh koh • mee • sah • reeyah duh
poh • lees*

There was an
accident/attack.
Il y a eu un accident/une attaque.
*eel • yah ew uhN nahk • see • dawN/ewn
ah • tahk*

My child is missing.
Mon enfant a disparu.
mohN nawN • fawN ah dees • pah • rew

I need an
to make a phone
call.
**J'ai besoin d'un interprète/de
téléphoner.**
*interpreter/zhay buh • zwehN
duhN nehN • tehr • preht/ duh
tay • lay • foh • nay*

I'm innocent.
Je suis innocent m/innocente f.
*zhuh swee zee • noh • sawN/
zee • noh • sawNt*

CRIME & LOST PROPERTY

I want to report…	**Je voudrais signaler…**
	zhuh voo • dray see • nyah • lay…
a mugging	**une attaque**
	ewn ah • tahk
a rape	**un viol**
	uhN veeyohl
a theft	**un vol**
	uhN vohl
I've been mugged.	**J'ai été attaqué** m **/attaquée** f.
	zhay ay • tay ah • tah • kay
I've been robbed.	**J'ai été dévalisé** m **/dévalisée** f.
	zhay ay • tay day • vah • lee • zay
I've lost…	**J'ai perdu…**
	zhay pehr • dew…
…was stolen.	**…a été vole** m **/volée** f.
	… ah ay • tay voh • lay
My backpack	**Mon sac-à-dos**
	mohN sahk • ah • doh
My bicycle	**Mon vélo**
	mohN vay • loh
My camera	**Mon appareil photo**
	mohN nah • pah • rehy foh • toh
My (hire) car	**Ma voiture (de location)**
	mah vwah • tuhr (duh loh • kah • seeyohN)
My computer	**Mon ordinateur**
	mohN nohr • dee • nah • tuhr
My credit card	**Ma carte de crédit**
	mah kahrt duh kray • dee
My jewelry	**Mes bijoux**
	may bee • zhoo
My money	**Mon argent**
	mohN nahr • zhawN

My passport	**Mon passeport**
	mohN pahs • pohr
My purse [handbag]	**Mon sac**
	mohN sahk
My traveller's cheques	**Mes chèques de voyage**
	may shehk duh vwah • yahzh
My wallet	**Mon porte-feuille**
	mohN pohrt • fuhy
I need a police report.	**J'ai besoin d'un constat de police.**
	zhay buh • zwehN duhN kohN • stah duh poh • lees
Where is the British/ American/Irish oo ay embassy?	**Où est l'ambassade britannique/ américaine/irlandaise ?**
	lawN • bah • sahd bree • tah • neek/ ah • may • ree • kayn/eer • lawN • dayz

HEALTH

NEED TO KNOW

I'm sick .	**Je suis malade.**
	zhuh swee mah • lahd
I need an English-speaking doctor.	**J'ai besoin d'un docteur qui parle anglais.**
	zhay buh • zwehN duhN dohk • tuhr kee pahrl awN • glay
It hurts here.	**Ça fait mal ici.**
	sah fay mahl ee • see

FINDING A DOCTOR

Can you recommend a doctor/dentist?	**Pouvez-vous me recommander un docteur/dentiste ?**
	poo • vay • voo muh ruh • koh • mawN • day uhN dohk • tuhr/dawN • teest
Can the doctor come here?	**Est-ce que le docteur peut venir ici ?**
	ehs kuh luh dohk • tuhr puh veh • neer ee • see
I need an English-speaking doctor.	**J'ai besoin d'un docteur qui parle anglais.**
	zhay buh • zwehN duhN dohk • tuhr kee pahrl awN • glay
What are the office hours?	**Quelles sont les heures d'ouverture ?**
	kehl sohN lay zuhr doo • vehr • tewr
I'd like an appointment for…	**Je voudrais un rendez-vous pour…**
	zhuh voo • dray uhN rawN • day-voo poor…
today	**aujourd'hui**
	oh • zhoor • dwee
tomorrow	**demain**
	duh • mehN
as soon as possible	**le plus vite possible**
	luh plew veet poh • see • bluh
It's urgent.	**C'est urgent.**
	say tewr • zhawN

SYMPTOMS

I'm bleeding.	**Je saigne.**
	zhuh sehnyuh
I'm constipated.	**Je suis constipé** *m*/**constipée** *f.*
	zhuh swee kohN • stee • pay

I'm dizzy.	**J'ai des vertiges.** *zhay day vehr • teezh*
I'm nauseous.	**J'ai des nausées.** *zhay day noh • zay*
I'm vomiting.	**Je vomis.** *zhuh voh • mee*
It hurts here.	**J'ai mal ici.** *zhay mahl ee • see*
I have…	**J'ai…** *zhay…*
an allergic reaction	**une réaction allergique** *ewn reh • ahk • seeyohN ah • lehr • zheek*
chest pain	**une douleur à la poitrine** *ewn doo • luhr ah lah pwah • treen*
cramps	**des crampes** *day krawNp*
diarrhea	**la diarrhée** *lah deeyah • ray*
an earache	**mal aux oreilles** *mahl oh zoh • rehy*
a fever	**de la fièvre** *duh lah feeyeh • vruh*
pain	**mal** *mahl*
a rash	**une irritation cutanée** *ewn ee • ree • tah • seeyohN kew • tah • nay*
a sprain	**une entorse** *ewn awN • tohrs*
some swelling	**une grosseur** *ewn groh • suhr*
a sore throat	**un mal de gorge** *uhN mahl duh gohrzh*
a stomachache	**mal au ventre** *mahl oh vawN • truh*

I've been sick for...days.

Je suis malade depuis...jours.
zhuh swee mah • lahd duh • pwee...zhoor

For Numbers, see page 20.

YOU MAY HEAR...

Qu'est-ce qui ne va pas ?
kehs kee nuh vah pah

What's wrong?

Où est-ce que ça fait mal ?
oo ehs kuh sah fay mahl

Where does it hurt?

Est-ce que ça fait mal ici ?
ehs kuh sah fay mahl ee • see

Does it hurt here?

Prenez-vous des médicaments ?
prueh • nay • voo day may • dee • kah • mawN

Are you on medication?

Êtes-vous allergique à quelque chose ?
eht • voo zah • lehr • zheek ah kehl • kuh shohz

Are you allergic to anything?

Ouvrez la bouche.
oo • vray lah boosh

Open your mouth.

Respirez profondément.
rehs • pee • ray proh • fohN • day • mawN

Breathe deeply.

Toussez, s'il vous plaît.
too • say seel voo play

Cough, please.

Allez à l'hôpital.
ah • lay ah loh • pee • tahl

Go to the hospital.

CONDITIONS

I'm…	**Je suis…**
	zhuh swee…
anemic	**anémique**
	ah • nay • meek
asthmatic	**asthmatique**
	ahs • mah • teek
diabetic	**diabétique**
	deeyah • bay • teek
epileptic	**épileptique** *ay • peel • ay • pteek*
I'm allergic to antibiotics/ penicillin.	**Je suis allergique aux antibiotiques/à la pénicilline.**
	zhuh swee zah • lehr • zheek oh zawN • tee • beeyoh • teek/ah lah pay • nee • see • leen
I have…	**J'ai…**
	zhay…
arthritis	**de l'arthrite**
	duh lahr • treet
a heart condition	**un problème cardiaque**
	uhN proh • blehm kahr • deeyahk
high/low blood pressure	**une tension élevée/basse**
	ewn tawN • seeyohN ay • luh • vay/bahs

I'm on…   **Je prends…**
          zhuh prawN…

TREATMENT

Do I need a prescription/medicine?

Ai-je besoin d'une ordonnance/de médicaments ?
ay•zhuh buh•zwehN dewn ohr•doh•nawNs/duh meh•dee•kah•mawN

Can you prescribe a generic drug [unbranded medication]?

Pouvez-vous me prescrire un médicament générique ?
poo•vay•voo muh prehs•kreer uhN may•dee•kah•mawN zhay•nay•reek

Where can I get it?

Où puis-je l'obtenir ?
oo pwee•zhuh lohb•tuh•neer

For Pharmacy, see page 154.

HOSPITAL

Notify my family, please.

Informez ma famille, s'il vous plaît.
ehN•fohr•may mah fah•meeyuh seel voo play

I'm in pain.   **J'ai mal.**
               zhay mahl

I need a doctor/nurse.

J'ai besoin d'un docteur/d'une infirmière.
zhay buh•zwehN duhN dohk•tuhr/dewn ehN•feer•meeyehr

When are visiting hours?

Quand sont les heures de visite ?
kawN sohN lay zuhr duh vee•zeet

I'm visiting…   **Je viens voir…**
                zhuh veeyehN vwahr…

DENTIST

I have...	**J'ai...**
	zhay...
a broken tooth	**une dent cassée**
	ewn dawN kah • say
a lost filling	**perdu un plombage**
	pehr • dew uhN plohN • bahzh
a toothache	**mal aux dents**
	mahl oh dawN
Can you fix this denture?	**Pouvez-vous réparer ce dentier ?**
	poo • vay • voo ray • pah • ray suh dawN • teeyay

GYNECOLOGIST

I have cramps/ a vaginal infection.	**J'ai des crampes/une infection vaginale.**
	zhay day krawNp/ewn ehN • fehk • seeyohN vah • zhee • nahl
I missed my period.	**Je n'ai pas eu mes règles.**
	zhuh nay pah ew may reh • gluh
I'm on the Pill.	**Je prends la pillule.**
	zhuh prawN lah pee • lewl
I'm (...months) pregnant.	**Je suis enceinte (de...mois).**
	zhuh swee zawN • sehNt (duh...mwah)
I'm not pregnant.	**Je ne suis pas enceinte.**
	zhuh nuh swee pah zawN • sehNt
My last period was...	**Mes dernières règles étaient...**
	may dehr • neeyehr reh • gluh ay • tay...

For Numbers, see page 20.

OPTICIAN

I've lost…	**J'ai perdu…**
	zhay pehr • dew…
a contact lens	**une lentille de contact**
	ewn lawN • tee • yuh duh kohN • tahk
my glasses	**mes lunettes**
	may lew • neht
a lens	**une lentille**
	ewn lawN • tee • yuh

PAYMENT & INSURANCE

How much?	**Combien ça coûte ?**
	kohN • beeyehN sah koot
Can I pay by credit card?	**Puis-je payer par carte ?**
	pwee • zhuh pay • yay pahr kahrt
I have insurance.	**J'ai une assurance.**
	zhay ewn ah • sew • rawNs
I need a receipt for my insurance.	**J'ai besoin d'un reçu pour ma compagnie d'assurance.**
	zhay buh • zwehN duhN ruh • sew poor mah kohN • pah • nee dah • sew • rawNs

PHARMACY

NEED TO KNOW

Where's the pharmacy?	**Où est la pharmacie ?**
	oo ay lah fahr • mah • see
What time does it open/close?	**À quelle heure ouvre-t-elle/ ferme-t-elle ?**
	ah kehl uhr oo • vruh • tehl/fehrm • tehl
What would you recommend for...?	**Que me conseillez-vous pour...?**
	kuh muh kohN • say • yay • voo poor...
How much do I take?	**Combien dois-je en prendre ?**
	kohN • beeyehN dwah • zhuh awN prawN • druh
I'm allergic to...	**Je suis allergique à...**
	zhuh swee zah • lehr • zheek ah...

WHAT TO TAKE

How much do I take?	**Combien dois-je en prendre ?** *kohN • beeyehN dwah • zhuh awN prawN • druh*
How often?	**Combien de fois ?** *kohN • beeyehN duh fwah*
Is it safe for children?	**Est-ce sans danger pour les enfants ?** *ehs sawN dawN • zay poor lay zawN • fawN*
I'm taking…	**Je prends…** *zhuh prawN…*
Are there side effects?	**Y-a-t-il des effets secondaires ?** *yah • teel day zeh • feh suh • kohN • dehr*
I need something for…	**J'ai besoin de quelque chose pour soigner…** *zhay buh • zwehN duh kehl • kuh shohz poor swah • nyay…*
a cold	**un rhume** *uhN rewm*
a cough	**une toux** *ewn too*
diarrhea	**une diarrhée** *ewn deeyah • ray*
a headache	**un mal de tête** *uhN mahl duh tayt*
insect bites	**des piqures d'insectes** *day pee • kewr dehN • sehkt*
motion sickness	**le mal des transports** *luh mahl day trawNs • pohr*
a sore throat	**un mal à la gorge** *uhN mahl ah lah gohrzh*
sunburn	**un coup de soleil** *uhN koo duh soh • lehy*

a toothache	**un mal de dents**
	uhN mahl duh dawN
an upset stomach	**un mal au ventre**
	uhN mahl oh vawN•truh

YOU MAY HEAR...

UNE/TROIS FOIS PAR JOUR	once/three times a day
UN CACHET	tablet
UNE GOUTTE	drop
UNE CUILLÈRE	teaspoon
...LES REPAS	...meals
APRÈS	after
AVANT	before
PENDANT	with
À JEUN	on an empty stomach
À AVALER	swallow whole
RISQUE DE SOMNOLENCE	may cause drowsiness
NE PAS AVALER	do not ingest

Pharmacies can be identified by the green cross-shaped neon light on display. Pharmacies are usually open from 9:00 a.m. to 6:00 p.m., without closing for lunch. Some pharmacies are open from 8:00 a.m. to 2:00 a.m. or even 24 hours, especially in the larger cities; a list of 24-hour pharmacies can be found on the door of every pharmacy. Some doctors still make house calls; ask your concierge for more information.

BASIC SUPPLIES

I'd like…	**Je voudrais…**
	zhuh voo • dray…
acetaminophen [paracetamol]	**du paracétamol**
	dew pah • rah • say • tah • mohl
antiseptic cream	**une crème antiseptique**
	ewn krehm awN • tee • sehp • teek
aspirin	**une aspirine**
	ewn ahs • pee • reen
bandages	**des pansements**
	day pawNs • mawN
a comb	**un peigne**
	uhN peh • nyuh
condoms	**des préservatifs**
	day pray • sehr • vah • teef
contact lens solution	**de la solution pour lentilles de contact**
	duh lah soh • lew • seeyohN poor lawN • tee • yuh duh kohN • tahk
deodorant	**du déodorant**
	dew day • oh • doh • rawN
a hairbrush	**une brosse à cheveux**
	ewn brohs ah shuh • vuh

hairspray	**de la laque**
	duh lah lahk
ibuprofen	**de l'ibuprofène**
	duh lee • bew • proh • fehn
insect repellent	**de la lotion anti-insectes**
	duh lah loh • seeyohN
	awN • tee • ehN • sehkt
lotion	**une lotion**
	ewn loh • seeyohN
a nail file	**une lime à ongle**
	ewn leem ah ohN • gluh
a (disposable)	**un rasoir (jetable)**
razor	*uhN rah • zwahr (zhuh • tah • bluh)*
razor blades	**des lames de rasoir**
	day lahm duh rah • zwahr
sanitary napkins	**des serviettes hygiéniques**
	day sehr • veeyeht [towels]
	ee • zheeyay • neek
shampoo/	**du shampooing/de l'après shampooing**
conditioner	*dew shawN • poo • wehN/duh lah • preh*
	shawN • poo • wehN
soap	**du savon**
	dew sah • vohN
sunscreen	**de la crème solaire**
	duh lah krehm soh • lehr
tampons	**des tampons**
	day tawN • pohN
tissues	**des Kleenex®**
	day klee • nehks
toilet paper	**du papier toilette**
	dew pah • peeyay twah • leht
toothpaste	**du dentifrice**
	dew dehN • tee • frees

For Baby Essentials, see page 138.

CHILD HEALTH & EMERGENCY

Can you recommend a pediatrician?	**Pouvez-vous me recommander un pédiatre ?**
	poo • vay • voo muh ruh • koh • mawN • day uhN pay • deeyah • truh
My child is allergic to…	**Mon enfant est allergique à…**
	mohN nawN • fawN ay ah • lehr • zheek ah…
My child is missing.	**Mon enfant a disparu.**
	mohN nawN • fawN ah dees • pah • rew
Have you seen a boy/girl?	**Avez-vous vu un garçon/une fille ?**
	ah • vay • voo vew uhN gahr • sohN/ewn fee • yuh

For Police, see page 144.

DISABLED TRAVELERS

NEED TO KNOW

Is there…?	**Y-a-t-il…?**
	yah • teel…
access for the disabled	**un accès pour handicapés**
	uhN nahk • seh poor
	awN • dee • kah • pay
a wheelchair ramp	**un accès pour chaises roulantes**
	uhN nahk • say poor shehz roo • lawNt
a disabled-toilet	**des toilettes accessibles aux handicapés**
	day twah • leht ahk • seh • see • bluh
accessible toilet	*oh zawN • dee • kah • pay*
I need…	**J'ai besoin…**
	zhay buh • zwehN…
assistance	**d'aide**
	dehd
an elevator [a lift]	**d'un ascenseur**
	duhN nah • sawN • suhr
a ground-floor room	**d'une chambre au rez-de-chaussée**
	dewn shawN • bruh oh
	ray • duh • shoh • say

ASKING FOR ASSISTANCE

I'm…	**Je suis…**
	zhuh swee…
disabled	**handicapé** *m*/**handicapée** *f*
	awN • dee • kah • pay

visually impaired	**malvoyant** m/**malvoyante** f
	mahl • vwah • yawN/mahl • vwah • yawNt
deaf	**sourd** m/**sourde** f
	soor/soord
hearing impaired	**malentendant** m/**malentendante** f
	mah • lawN • tawN • dawN/
	mah • lawN • tawN • dahNt
unable to walk far/use the stairs	**incapable de marcher longtemps/ d'utiliser les escaliers**
	ehN • kah • pah • bluh duh mahr • shay lohN • tawN/dew • tee • lee • zay lay zehs • kah • leeyay
Please speak louder.	**S'il vous plaît, parlez plus fort.**
	seel voo play pahr • lay plew fohr
Can I bring my wheelchair?	**Puis-je apporter ma chaise roulante ?**
	pwee • zhuh ah • pohr • tay mah shehz roo • lawNt
Are guide dogs permitted?	**Est-ce que les chiens de guide sont autorisés ?**
	ehs kuh lay sheeyehN duh geed sohN toh • toh • ree • zay
Can you help me?	**Pouvez-vous m'aider ?**
	poo • vay • voo mehy • day
Please open/hold the door.	**S'il vous plaît, ouvrez/tenez la porte.**
	seel voo play oo • vray/tuh • nay lah pohrt

FOOD

EATING OUT	164
MEALS & COOKING	175
DRINKS	197
ON THE MENU	204

EATING OUT

NEED TO KNOW

Can you recommend a good restaurant/bar?
Pouvez-vous me conseiller un bon restaurant/bar ?
poo • vay-voo muh kohN • say • yay uhN bohN reh • stoh • rawN/bahr

Is there a traditional French/an inexpensive restaurant nearby?
Y-a-t-il un restaurant traditionnel français/bon marché près d'ici ?
yah • teel uhN reh • stoh • rawN trah • dee • seeyohN • nehl frawN • say/bohN mahr • shay pray dee • see

A table for..., please.
Une table pour..., s'il vous plaît.
ewn tah • bluh poor…seel voo play

Can we sit...?
Pouvons-nous nous asseoir...?
poo • vohN-noo noo zah • swahr…

   here/there
ici/là
ee • see/lah

   outside
dehors
duh • ohr

   in a non-smoking area
en zone non-fumeur
awN zohn nohN-few • muhr

I'm waiting for someone.
J'attends quelqu'un.
zhah • tawN kehl • kuhN

Where are the toilets?
Où sont les toilettes?
oo sohN lay twah • leht

A menu, please.
La carte, s'il vous plaît.
lah kahrt seel voo play

What do you
Que recommandez-vous ?

recommend?	*kuh reh • koh • mawN • day-voo*
I'd like…	**Je voudrais…**
	zhuh voo • dray…
Some more…, please.	**Un peu plus de…, s'il vous plaît.**
	uhN puh plew duh…seel voo play
Enjoy your meal!	**Bon appétit !**
	bohN nah • peh • tee
The check [bill], please.	**L'addition, s'il vous plaît.**
	lah • dee • seeyohN seel voo play
Is service included?	**Est-ce que le service est compris ?**
	ehs kuh luh sehr • vees ay kohN • pree
Can I pay by credit card/have a receipt?	**Puis-je payer par carte de crédit/ avoir un reçu ?**
	pwee • zhuh pay • yay pahr kahrt duh kray • dee/ah • vwahr uhN ruh • sew

WHERE TO EAT

Can you recommend…?	**Pouvez-vous me conseiller…?**
	poo • vay • voo muh kohN • say • yay…
a restaurant	**un restaurant**
	uhN reh • stoh • rawN
a bar	**un bar**
	uhN bahr
a café	**un café**
	uhN kah • fay
a fast-food place	**un fast-food**
	uhN fahst • food
a cheap restaurant	**un restaurant bon marché**
	uhN reh • stoh • rawN bohN mahr • shay
an expensive restaurant	**un restaurant cher**
	uhN reh • stoh • rawN shehr

a restaurant with a good view	**un restaurant avec belle vue**
	uhN reh • stoh • rawN ah • vehk behl vew
an authentic/ a non-touristy restaurant	**un restaurant authentique/qui n'est pas envahi par les touristes**
	uhN reh • stoh • rawN oh • tawN • teek / kee nay pah awN • vah • yee pahr lay too • reest

RESERVATIONS & PREFERENCES

I'd like to reserve a table...	**Je voudrais réserver une table...**
	zhuh voo • dray ray • zehr • vay ewn tah • bluh...
or two	**pour deux**
	poor duh
for this evening	**pour ce soir**
	poor suh swahr
for tomorrow at...	**pour demain à...**
	poor duh • mehN ah...
A table for two, please.	**Une table pour deux, s'il vous plaît.**
	ewn tah • bluh poor duh seel voo play
I have a reservation.	**J'ai une réservation.**
	zhay ewn ray • zehr • vah • seeyohN
My name is...	**Mon nom est...**
	mohN nohN ay...

Can we sit…?	**Pouvons-nous nous asseoir…?**
	poo • vohN • noo noo zah • swahr…
here/there	**ici/là**
	ee • see/lah
outside	**dehors**
	duh • ohr
in a non-smoking area	**en zone non-fumeur**
	awN zohn nohN • few • muhr
by the window	**à côté de la fenêtre**
	ah koh • tay duh lah fuh • neh • truh
in the shade	**à l'ombre**
	ah lohN • bruh
in the sun	**au soleil**
	oh soh • lehy
Where are the toilets?	**Où sont les toilettes ?**
	oo sohN lay twah • leht

YOU MAY HEAR…

Avez-vous réservé ?	Do you have a reservation?
ah • vay • voo ray • zehr • vay	
Pour combien?	How many?
poor kohN • beeyehN	
Fumeur ou non-fumeur?	Smoking or non-smoking?
few • muhr oo nohN • few • muhr	
Êtes-vous prêts (à commander) ?	Are you ready (to order)?
eht • voo preh (ah koh • mawN • day)	
Que désirez-vous?	What would you
kuh day • zee • ray • voo like?	
Je vous conseille…	I recommend…
zhuh voo kohN • sehy…	
Bon appétit.	Enjoy your meal.
bohN nah • peh • tee	

HOW TO ORDER

Excuse me, sir /ma'am?	**S'il vous plaît, monsieur/madame ?** *seel voo play muh • seeyuhr/mah • dahm*
We're ready (to order).	**Nous sommes prêts (à commander).** *noo sohm preh (ah koh • mawN • day)*
May I see the wine list?	**La liste des vins, s'il vous plaît.** *lah leest day vehN seel voo play*
I'd like…	**Je voudrais…** *zhuh voo • dray…*
a bottle of…	**une bouteille de…** *ewn boo • tehy duh…*
a carafe of…	**une carafe de…** *ewn kah • rahf duh…*
a glass of…	**un verre de…** *uhN vehr duh…*
Can I have a menu?	**La carte, s'il vous plaît.** *lah kahrt seel voo play*
Do you have…?	**Avez-vous…?** *ah • vay voo…*
a fixed-price menu	**un menu à prix fixe** *uhN muh • new ah pree feeks*
a menu in English	**un menu en anglais** *uhN muh • new awN nawN • glay*
a children's menu	**un menu enfant** *uhN muh • new awN • fawN*
What do you recommend?	**Que me conseillez-vous ?** *kuh muh kohN • say • yay • voo*
What's this?	**Qu'est-ce que c'est ?** *kehs kuh say*
What's in it?	**Quels sont les ingrédients ?** *kehl sohN lay zehN • gray • deeyehN*
Is it spicy?	**C'est épicé ?** *say ay • pee • say*

I'd like…	**Je voudrais…**	
	zhuh voo • dray…	
More…, please.	**Plus…, s'il vous plaît.**	
	plews…seel voo play	
With/Without…	**Avec/Sans…**	
	ah • vehk/sawN…	
I can't eat…	**Je ne peux pas manger…**	
	zhuh nuh puh pah mawN • zhay…	
rare	**saignant**	
	say • nyawN	
medium	**à point**	
	ah pwehN	
well-done	**bien cuit**	
	beeyehN kwee	
It's to go [take away].	**C'est pour emporter.**	
	say poor awN • pohr • tay	

For Drinks, see page 197.

YOU MAY SEE…

COUVERT	cover charge
PRIX FIXE	fixed-price
MENU (DU JOUR)	menu (of the day)
SERVICE (NON) COMPRIS	service (not) included
MENU À LA CARTE	specials

COOKING METHODS

baked	**cuit**
	kwee
boiled	**bouilli**
	boo • yee
braised	**braisé**
	bray • zay
breaded	**en croute**
	awN kroot
creamed	**à la crème**
	ah lah krehm
diced	**en rondelles**
	awN rohN • dehl
filleted	**en filets**
	awN fee • lay
fried	**frit**
	free
grilled	**grillé**
	gree • yay
poached	**poché**
	poh • shay
roasted	**rôti**
	roh • tee

sautéed	**poêlé**
	pwah • lay
smoked	**fumé**
	few • may
steamed	**à la vapeur**
	ah lah vah • puhr
stewed	**mijoté**
	mee • zhoh • tay
stuffed	**farci**
	fahr • see

DIETARY REQUIREMENTS

I'm...	**Je suis...**
	zhuh swee...
diabetic	**diabétique**
	deeyah • beh • teek
lactose intolerant	**allergique au lactose**
	ah • lehr • zheek oh lahk • tohz
vegetarian	**végétarien** *m*/**végétarienne** *f*
	vay • zhay • tah • reeyehN/
	vay • zhay • tah • reeyehn
vegan	**végétalien** *m*/ **végétalienne** *f*
	vay • zhay • tah • leeyehN/
	vay • zhay • tah • leeyehn
I'm allergic to...	**Je suis allergique à...**
	zhuh swee ah • lehr • zheek ah...
I can't eat...	**Je ne peux pas manger...**
	zhuh nuh puh pah mawN • zhay...
dairy products	**de produits laitiers**
	duh proh • dwee lay • teeyay
gluten	**de gluten**
	duh glew • tawN
nuts	**des noix**
	day nwah

pork	**du porc**
	dew pohr
shellfish	**des fruits de mer**
	day frwee duh mehr
spicy foods	**de la nourriture épicée**
	duh lah noo • ree • tewr ay • pee • say
wheat	**du blé**
	dew blay
Is it halal/kosher?	**Est-ce que c'est halal/casher ?**
	ehs kuh say ah • lahl/kah • shehr
Do you have...?	**Avez-vous...?**
	ah • vay voo...
skimmed milk	**du lait écrémé**
	dew lay ay • kray • may
whole milk	**du lait entier**
	dew lay awN • teeyay
soya milk	**du lait de soja**
	dew lay duh soh • zhah

DINING WITH CHILDREN

Do you have children's portions?	**Faites-vous des portions enfants ?**
	feht • voo day pohr • seeyohN awN • fawN
Can I have a highchair/child's seat?	**Une chaise haute pour bébé/Un siège pour enfant, s'il vous plaît.**
	ewn shay zoht poor bay • bay/uhN seeyehzh poo rawN • fawN seel voo play
Where can I feed/change the baby?	**Où puis-je allaiter/changer le bébé ?**
	oo pwee • zhuh ah • leh • tay/shawN • zhay luh bay • bay
Can you warm this?	**Pouvez-vous réchauffer ceci ?**
	poo • vay • voo ray • shoh • fay suh • see

For Traveling with Children, see page 136.

HOW TO COMPLAIN

When will our food be ready?	**Dans combien de temps serons-nous servis ?**
	dawN kohN • beeyehN duh tawN suh • rohN • noo sehr • vee
We can't wait any longer.	**Nous ne pouvons plus attendre.**
	noo nuh poo • vohN plew zhah • tawN • druh
We're leaving.	**Nous partons.**
	noo pahr • tohN
I didn't order this.	**Ce n'est pas ce que j'ai commandé.**
	suh nay pah suh kuh zhay koh • mawN • day
I ordered…	**J'ai commandé…**
	zhay koh • mawN • day…
I can't eat this.	**Je ne peux pas manger ça.**
	zhuh nuh puh pah mawN • zhay sah
This is too…	**C'est trop…**
	say troh…
cold/hot	**froid/chaud**
	frwah/shoh
salty/spicy	**salé/épicé**
	sah • lay/ay • pee • say
tough/bland	**dur/sans goût**
	dewr/sawN goo
This isn't clean/fresh.	**Ce n'est pas propre/frais.**
	suh nay pah proh • pruh/fray

PAYING

The check [bill], please.	**L'addition, s'il vous plaît.**
	lah • dee • seeyohN seel voo play
Separate checks day [bills], please.	**Des additions séparées, s'il vous plaît.**
	zah • dee • seeyohN say • pah • ray seel voo play

It's all together.	**C'est ensemble.**
	say tawN • sawN • bluh
Is service included?	**Le service est-il compris ?**
	luh sehr • vees ay • teel kohN • pree
What's this amount for?	**À quoi correspond ce montant ?**
	ah kwah koh • rhes • pohN suh mohN • tawN
I didn't have that. I had…	**Je n'ai pas eu ceci. J'ai eu…**
	zhuh nay pah ew suh • see zhay ew…
Can I have a receipt/ an itemized bill?	**Puis-je avoir un reçu/reçu détaillé ?**
	pwee • zhuh ah • vwahr uhN ruh • sew/ ruh • sew day • tie • yay
That was delicious!	**C'était délicieux !**
	seh • tay day • lee • seeyuh
I've already paid.	**J'ai déjà payé.**
	zhay day • zhah pay • yay

Service is included in the price at cafes and restaurants. However, people do tend to leave a small tip. Round up the bill to the nearest euro or two for good service.

MEALS & COOKING

BREAKFAST

le bacon   bacon
luh beh•kohn
le beurre   butter
luh buhr
le café/thé...   coffee/tea...
luh kah•fay/tay...
  noir   black
  nwahr
  déca   decaf
  day•kah
  au lait   with milk
  oh lay
  avec du sucre   with sugar
  ah•vehk dew sew•kruh
  avec de l'édulcorant   with artificial
  ah•vehk duh lay•dewl•koh•rawN   sweetener
les céréales chaudes/froides   cold/hot cereal
lay say•ray•ahl shohd/frwahd
la charcuterie   cold cuts
lah shahr•kew•tuh•ree
le croissant   croissant
luh krwah•sawN
la confiture   jam/jelly
lah kohN•fee•tewr
le fromage   cheese
luh froh•mahzh
le jus...   ...juice
luh zhew...
  d'orange   orange
  doh•rawNzh

de pommes *duh pohm*	apple
de pamplemousse *duh pawN•pluh•moos*	grapefruit
le lait *luh lay*	milk
l'avoine *lah•vwahn*	oatmeal
l'eau *loh*	water
le muesli *luh mews•lee*	granola [muesli]
le muffin *luh muh•feen*	muffin
l'œuf… *luhf…*	…egg
dur/à la coque *dewr/ah lah kohk*	hard-/soft-boiled
sur le plat *sewr luh plah*	fried
brouillé *broo•yay*	scrambled
l'omelette *lohm•leht*	omelet

le pain	bread
luh pehN	
le pain grillé	toast
luh pehN gree•yay	
le petit pain	roll
luh puh•tee pehN	
la saucisse	sausage
lah soh•sees	
le yaourt	yogurt
luh yah•oort	

Le petit déjeuner (breakfast) is usually served from 7:00 a.m. until 10:00 a.m. and is a light meal, such as bread with butter and jam and coffee or tea. **Le déjeuner** (lunch) is usually served from noon until 2:00 p.m. and can be a full sit-down meal or a fast meal on the go, whichever you have time for. A picnic lunch is popular, and all the fixings can be found at the local bakery, butcher and wine store. **Le goûter** (snack), perhaps a croissant or pieces of chocolate, is common in the afternoon, especially for children. **Le dîner** (dinner) is usually served between 7:00 p.m. and 10:00 p.m. This often is a multi-course meal, served with wine, and enjoyed at a leisurely pace.

APPETIZERS

les acras	small, fried fritters made from cod
lay zhah•krah	
l'andouille	seasoned sausage, served grilled or fried
lawN•doohy	

la bouchée à la reine
lah boo • shay ah lah rehn

pastry shell filled with creamed sweetbreads and mushrooms

les crudités variées
lay krew • dee • tay vah • reeyay

assorted vegetables in a vinaigrette dressing

les escargots
lay zehs • kahr • goh

snails

le foie gras
luh fwah grah

fresh goose liver

le pâté
luh pah • tay

liver paté

les quenelles
lay kuh • nehl

light dumplings made of fish, fowl or meat, in cream sauce

les quenelles de brochet
lay kuh • nehl duh broh • shay

dumplings made of pike in cream sauce

la quiche
lah keesh

an open-faced egg and cheese tart filled with vegetables, meat or seafood

la quiche lorraine
lah keesh loh • rayn

open-faced egg and cheese tart filled with bacon

les rillettes
lay ree • yeht

pork mixture served as a spread for bread

la terrine
lah teh • reen

pâté made from pork, poultry, game or fish

les toasts
lay tohst

toasted pieces of bread with different toppings

SOUP

l'aïgo boulido
lah • ee • goh boolee • doh
garlic soup, a specialty of Provence

la bisque
lah beesk
seafood stew

la bouillabaisse
lah boo • yah • behs
seafood soup, a specialty of Marseilles

le consommé
luh kohN • soh • may
clear soup

le consommé Célestine
luh kohN • soh • may say • lehs • teen
clear soup with chicken and noodles

le consommé Colbert
luh kohN • soh • may kohl • behr
clear soup with poached eggs, spring vegetables

le consommé à l'œuf
luh kohN • soh • may ah luhf
clear soup with a raw egg

le consommé au porto
luh kohN • soh • may oh pohr • toh
clear soup with port wine

la garbure
lah gahr • bewr
cabbage soup, often with pork or goose

le potage à l'ail
luh poh • tahzh ah lie
garlic soup

le potage du barry
luh poh • tahzh dew bah • ree
cream of cauliflower soup

le potage bilibi
luh poh • tahzh bee • lee • bee
fish and oyster soup

le potage bonne ferme
luh poh • tahzh bohn fehrm
soup with potatoes, leeks and sometimes bacon

le potage condé
luh poh • tahzh kohN • day
soup with mashed red beans

le potage crécy
luh poh • tahzh kray • see

soup with carrots and rice

le potage au cresson
luh poh • tahzh oh kreh • sohN

watercress soup

le potage julienne
luh poh • tahzh zhew • leeyehn

shredded vegetable soup

le potage Parmentier
luh poh • tahzh pahr • mawN • teeyay

potato soup

le pot-au-feu
luh poh-toh-fuh

meat and vegetable stew

le ragoût
luh rah • goo

thick stew

la soupe à la bière
lah soop ah lah beeyehr

beer soup with chicken stock and onions

la soupe aux choux
lah soop oh shoo

cabbage soup

la soupe de haricots
lah soop duh ah • ree • koh

bean soup

la soupe aux légumes
lah soop oh lay • gewm

vegetable soup

la soupe à l'oignon
lah soop ah loh • nyohN

French onion soup

la soupe au pistou
lah soop oh pees • too

basil-vegetable soup, a specialty of Provence

la soupe de poulet
lah soop duh poo • lay

chicken soup

la soupe de poisson
lah soop duh pwah • sohN

soup with small fish, simmered and pureed

la soupe de tomates
lah soop duh toh • maht

tomato soup

la soupe de volaille
lah soop duh voh • lie

chicken soup

le velouté
luh vuh • loo • tay

cream soup

FISH & SEAFOOD

le anchois
luh awN • shwah

anchovy

l'anguille
lawN • geeyuh

eel

le bar
luh bahr

bass

le bar aux herbes en chemise
luh bah roh zayrb awN sheh • meez

bass stuffed with spinach and herbs, wrapped in lettuce and poached in white wine

le brochet
luh broh • shay

pike

le calmar
luh kahl • mahr

squid

les coquilles Saint-Jacques
lay koh • keeyuh sehN • zhahk

breaded scallops sautéed in lemon juice and herbs

le crabe
luh krahb

crab

la crevette
lah kruh • veht

shrimp

la dorade
lah doh • rahd

sea bass

l'écrevisse
lay • kruh • vees

crawfish

l'escargot
lehs • kahr • goh

snail

l'espadon
leh • spah • dohN

swordfish

le flétan
luh flay • tawN

halibut

le hareng
luh ah • rawN

herring

le homard
luh oh • mahr

lobster

le homard cardinal
luh oh • mahr kahr • dee • nahl

lobster cooked with
mushrooms
and truffles in a
béchamel sauce

l'huître
luh wee • truh

oyster

la morue
lah moh • rew

cod

la moule
lah mool

mussel

les moules marinières
lay mool mah • ree • neeyehr

mussels in white
wine sauce

la palourde
lah pah • loord

clam

le plateau de fruits de mer
luh plah • toh duh frwee duh mehr

assorted seafood
platter

le poulpe	octopus
luh poolp	
la sardine	sardine
lah sahr•deen	
le saumon	salmon
luh soh•mohN	
le saumon à l'oseille	salmon with sorrel
luh soh•mohN ah loh•zehy	sauce
la sole	sole
lah sohl	
le thon	tuna
luh tohN	
la truite	trout
lah trweet	
la truite aux amandes	trout sautéed in a
lah trweet oh zah•mawNd	creamy almond
	sauce
la truite meunière	seasoned, breaded
lah trweet muh•neeyehr	trout, pan-fried in
	butter

MEAT & POULTRY

l'agneau	lamb
lah•nyoh	
le bacon	bacon
luh beh•kohn	
le bifteck	steak
luh beef•tehk	
le bœuf	beef
luh buhf	
la caille	quail
lah kie	
le canard	duck
luh kah•nahr	

le canard à l'orange
luh kah • nahr ah loh • rawNzh
duck braised with orange liqueur

le cassoulet toulousain
luh kah • soo • lay too • loo • zehN
casserole of white beans, mutton or salt pork, sausage and preserved goose

le cervela
luh sehr • vuh • lah
garlic pork sausage

le chevreuil
luh shuh • vruhy
venison

le cochon de lait
luh koh • shohN duh lay
suckling pig

le coq au vin
luh koh koh vehN
chicken in red wine sauce

la côtelette de porc
lah koh • tuh • leht duh pohr
pork chop

la dinde
lah dehNd
turkey

l'épaule d'agneau farcie
lay • pohl dah • nyoh fahr • see
stuffed lamb shoulder

l'escalope de veau normande
ehs • kah • lohp duh voh nohr • mawNd
thinly sliced veal in cream sauce

l'escalope de veau milanaise
lehs • kah • lohp duh voh mee • lah • nehz
thinly sliced veal in tomato sauce

le faisan
luh fay • zawN
pheasant

le foie
luh fwah
liver

le jambon
luh zhawN • bohN
ham

le lapin
luh lah • pehN
rabbit

le lapin à la Lorraine
luh lah • pehN ah lah loh • rehn
rabbit in a mushroom cream sauce

le lapin à la moutarde   rabbit in mustard
luh lah • pehN ah lah moo • tahrd   sauce
les lardons   cubes of salt pork
lay lahr • dohN
le porc   pork
luh pohr
le poulet   chicken
luh poo • lay
le poulet à l'estragon   chicken in a tarragon
luh poo • lay ah lehs • trah • gohN   cream sauce
le poulet chasseur   chicken in a
luh poo • lay shah • suhr   mushroom wine
    sauce
le ris   sweetbreads
luh rees
la saucisse   sausage
lah soh • sees
le steak   steak
luh stayk
le tournedos   small filet of beef
luh toor • nuh • doh
le veau   veal
luh voh

VEGETABLES & STAPLES

l'ail   garlic
lie
l'artichaut   artichoke
lahr • tee • shoh
les asperges   asparagus
lay zah • spehrzh
l'aubergine   eggplant [aubergine]
loh • behr • zheen

l'avocat
lah • voh • kah

avocado

le brocoli
luh broh • koh • lee

broccoli

la carotte
lah kah • roht

carrot

les carottes vichy
lay kah • roht vee • shee

carrots sauteed in butter

le céleri
luh say • luh • ree

celery

le champignon
luh shawN • pee • nyohN

mushroom

le chou
luh shoo

cabbage

les choux verts à l'anglaise
lay shoo vehr ah lawN • glehz

julienned cabbage, sautéed in butter

le chou-fleur
luh shoo • fluhr

cauliflower

le chou-fleur au gratin
luh shoo • fluhr oh grah • tehN

baked cauliflower, covered in cheese

la courgette
lah koor • zheht

zucchini [courgette]

les épinards
lay zay • pee • nahr

spinach

les épinards à la crème creamed spinach
lay zay • pee • nahr ah lah krehm

les haricots beans
lay ah • ree • koh

les haricots verts green beans
lay ah • ree • koh vehr

la laitue lettuce
lah lay • tew

les légumes vegetables
lay lay • gewm

le maïs corn
luh mah • ees

l'oignon onion
loh • nyohN

l'olive olive
loh • leev

les pâtes pasta
lay paht

les petits pois peas
lay puh • tee pwah

le poivron rouge/vert red/green pepper
roozh/ luh pwah • vrohN vehr

les poivrons farcis stuffed green
lay pwah • vrohN fahr • see peppers

la pomme de terre potato
lah pohm duh tehr

salade... salad...
sah • lahd...

  antiboise with anchovy, green
  ahN • tee • bwahz pepper, beets, rice
   and capers

  niçoise with tuna, anchovy,
  nee • swahz olives and
   vegetables

russe *rews*	with diced vegetables
de thon *duh tohN*	with tuna
verte *vehrt*	with mixed greens
le riz *luh ree*	rice
la tomate *lah toh • maht*	tomato

FRUIT

l'abricot *lah • bree • koh*	apricot
l'ananas *lah • nah • nah*	pineapple
la banane *lah bah • nahn*	banana
le cassis *luh kah • sees*	black currant
la cerise *lah suh • reez*	cherry
le citron *luh see • trohN*	lemon
le citron vert *luh see • trohN vehr*	lime
la fraise *lah frehz*	strawberry
la framboise *lah frawN • bwahz*	raspberry
le fruit *luh frwee*	fruit
la groseille *lah groh • zehy*	red currant

le melon	melon
luh muh • lohN	
la myrtille	blueberry
lah meer • teeyuh	
l'orange	orange
loh • rawNzh	
le pamplemousse	grapefruit
luh pawN • pluh • moos	
la pêche	peach
lah pehsh	
la poire	pear
lah pwahr	
la pomme	apple
lah pohm	
la prune	plum
lah prewn	
le raisin	grape
luh reh • zehN	

CHEESE

le banon	mild goat's and
luh bah • nohN	cow's milk cheese
	with a nutty flavor

le bleu d'auvergne
luh bluh doh • vehr • nyuh
cow's milk blue cheese with a strong flavor

le brie
luh bree
soft cheese, ranging in strength and flavors

le camembert
luh kah • mawN • behr
soft, raw cow's milk cheese

le coulommiers
luh koo • luh • meeyay
soft, mild cow's milk cheese

la fondue
lah fohN • dew
a pot of melted cheese dip

le fromage
luh froh • mahzh
cheese

le fromage blanc
luh froh • mahzh blawN
rich, creamy white eaten for breakfast topped cheese with cream and sugar

le fromage de chèvre
luh froh • mahzh duh sheh • vruh
goat's milk cheese

le munster
luh muhN • stuhr
soft, spicy cow's milk cheese from Alsace

le roquefort
luh rohk • fohr
blue, soft and pungent sheep's milk cheese

le Saint-Paulin
luh sehN • poh • lehN
smooth and mild cow's milk cheese

DESSERT

la crêpe...
lah krehp...
thin pancake...

   à la confiture
   ah lah kohN • fee • tewr
with jam

au sucre
oh sew • kruh

with sugar

suzette
sew • zeht

in an orange-flavored sauce

le beignet
luh beh • nyay

deep fried dough

le diplomate
luh dee • ploh • maht

molded custard with fruit, lined with sponge cake that has been steeped in liqueur

le gâteau au fromage
luh gah • toh oh froh • mahzh

cheesecake

la génoise
lah zhay • nwahz

sponge cake

le mont-blanc
luh mohN • blawN

pastry with chestnut purée, whipped cream and meringue

la mousse au chocolat
lah moos oh shoh • koh • lah

chocolate mousse

les petits fours
lay pu • tee foor

bite-sized, decorated pastries

la poire belle-hélène
lah pwahr behl • ehl • ehn

poached pears with ice cream and chocolate sauce

le sabayon
luh sah • bah • yohN

creamy dessert made from egg yolks, wine, sugar and flavoring

la tarte aux fruits
lah tahrt oh frwee

fruit pie or tart

la tarte tatin
lah tahrt tah • tehN

upside down baked apple tart

SAUCES & CONDIMENTS

à la bonne femme
ah lah bohn fehm

white wine sauce
with vegetables

béarnaise
beh • ahr • nehz

a sauce made with
butter, eggs, shallots,
wine and tarragon

bordelaise
bohr • duh • lehz

sauce made with
Bordeaux wine

chantilly
shawN • tee • yee

sauce made with
whipping cream

estragon
eh • strah • gohN

with tarragon

florentine
floh • rawN • teen

with spinach

hollandaise
oh • lawN • dehz

creamy egg yolk and
butter sauce

normande
nohr • mawNd

fish sauce with
shrimp or oysters

rémoulade
ray • moo • lahd

mayonnaise mixed
with mustard

sel
sehl

salt

poivre   pepper
pwah • vruh
moutarde   mustard
moo • tahrd
ketchup   ketchup
Ket • shuhp

AT THE MARKET

Where are the trolleys/baskets?	**Où sont les chariots/paniers ?** *oo sohN lay shah • reeyoh/pah • neeyay*
Where is...?	**Où est...?** *oo ay...*
I'd like some of that/this.	**Je voudrais un peu de cela/ceci.** *zhuh voo • dray zuhN puh duh suh • lah/ suh • see*
Can I taste it?	**Puis-je goûter ?** *pwee • zhuh goo • tay*
I'd like...	**Je voudrais...** *zhuh voo • dray...*
a kilo/half-kilo of...	**un kilo/demi-kilo de...** *uhN kee • loh/ duh • mee • kee • loh duh...*
a liter of...	**un litre de...** *uhN lee • truh duh...*
a piece of...	**une pièce de...** *ewn peeyehs duh...*
a slice of...	**un morceau de...** *uhN mohr • soh duh...*
More./Less.	**Plus./Moins.** *plews/mwehN*
How much?	**Combien ça coûte ?** *kohN • beeyehN sah koot*
Where do I pay?	**Où dois-je payer ?** *oo dwah • zhuh pay • yay*

A bag, please.	**Un sachet, s'il vous plaît.** *uhN sah • shay seel voo play*
I'm being helped.	**On me sert.** *ohN muh sehr*

For Paying & Bargaining, see page 109.

YOU MAY HEAR...

Puis-je vous aider?
pwee • zhuh voo zay • day

Can I help you?

Que voulez-vous?
kuh voo • lay • voo

What would you like?

Autre chose?
oh • truh shohz

Anything else?

Ça fait...euros.
Sah fay...uh • roh

That's...euros.

Local markets—indoor and outdoor—are a wonderful way to discover fresh, seasonal and regional products and to get a hint of the French way of life. Both sell a variety of products such as cheese, meat, flowers, homemade preserves, honey, nuts and farm fresh vegetables, fruit, eggs and more.

Measurements in Europe are metric—and that applies to the weight of food too. If you tend to think in pounds and ounces, it's worth brushing up on what the metric equivalent is before you go shopping for fruit and veg in markets and supermarkets. Five hundred grams, or half a kilo, is a common quantity to order, and that converts to just over a pound (17.65 ounces, to be precise).

IN THE KITCHEN

bottle opener	**un décapsuleur** *uhN day • kahp • sew • luhr*
bowl	**un saladier** *uhN sah • lah • deeyay*
can opener	**un ouvre-boîte** *uhN oo • vruh • bwaht*
corkscrew	**un tire-bouchon** *uhN teer • boo • shohN*
cup	**une tasse** *ewn tahs*
fork	**une fourchette** *ewn foor • sheht*
frying pan	**une poêle** *ewn pwahl*
glass	**un verre** *uhN vehr*
(steak) knife	**un couteau (à steak)** *uhN koo • toh (ah stayk)*
measuring cup/ spoon	**une mesure/cuillère à doser** *ewn meh • zewr/kwee • yehr ah doh • say*
napkin	**une serviette** *ewn sayr • veeyeht*

plate	**une assiette**
	ewn ah • seeyeht
pot	**une casserole**
	ewn kah • suh • rohl
spatula	**une spatule**
	ewn spah • tewl
spoon	**une cuillère**
	ewn kwee • yehr

YOU MAY SEE…

À CONSOMMER DE PRÉFÉRENCE AVANT LE…	best if used by…
KILOCALORIES	calories
0% DE MATIÈRES GRASSES	fat free
CONSERVER AU RÉFRIGÉRATEUR	keep refrigerated
PEUT CONTENIR DES TRACES DE…	may contain traces of…
VA AU MICRO-ONDE	microwaveable
DATE LIMITE DE VENTE…	sell by…
CONVIENT AUX VÉGÉTARIENS	suitable for vegetarians

DRINKS

NEED TO KNOW

Can I see the wine list /drinks menu, please?	**La carte des vins/ boissons, s'il vous plaît.** *lah kahrt day vehN/bwah • sohN seel voo play*
What do you recommend?	**Que me conseillez-vous ?** *kuh muh kohN • say • yay • voo*
I'd like a bottle/glass of red/white wine.	**Je voudrais une bouteille/un verre de vin rouge/blanc.** *zhuh voo • dray ewn boo • tehy/uhN vehr duh vehN roozh/blawN*
The house wine, please.	**Le vin de la maison, s'il vous plaît.** *luh vehN duh lah may • zohN seel voo play*
Another bottle/ glass, please.	**Une autre bouteille/Un autre verre, s'il vous plaît.** *ewn oh • truh boo • tehy/uhN noh • truh vehr seel voo play*
I'd like a local beer.	**Je voudrais une bière locale.** *zhuh voo • dray ewn beeyehr loh • kahl*
Can I buy you a drink?	**Puis-je vous offrir un verre ?** *pwee • zhuh voo zoh • freer uhN vehr*
Cheers!	**Santé !** *sawN • tay*
A coffee/tea, please.	**Un café/thé, s'il vous plaît.** *uhN kah • fay/tay seel voo play*
Black.	**Noir.** *nwahr*
With…	**Avec…** *ah • vehk…*

milk	**du lait**
	dew lay
sugar	**du sucre**
	dew sew • kruh
artificial sweetener	**de l'édulcorant**
	duh lay • dewl • koh • rawN
A…, please.	**Un…, s'il vous plaît.**
	uhN…seel voo play
juice	**jus de fruit**
	zhew duh frwee
soda	**soda**
	soh • dah
Sparkling/still water.	**De l'eau gazeuse/plate.**
	duh loh gah • zuhz/plaht

NON-ALCOHOLIC DRINKS

le café	coffee
luh kah • fay	
le chocolat chaud	hot chocolate
luh shoh • koh • lah shoh	
la citronnade	lemonade
lah see • troh • nahd	
l'eau gazeuse/plate	sparkling/still water
loh gah • zuhz/plaht	
le jus de fruit	juice
luh zhew duh frwee	
le lait	milk
luh lay	
le soda	soda
luh soh • dah	
le thé (glacé)	(iced) tea
luh tay (glah • say)	

France offers a wide choice of mineral water. Popular French brands include Evian®, Vittel®, Volvic® and Badoit®; Perrier® and Vichy® are popular sparkling waters. **Café** (espresso-style coffee) is also very popular. **Café** in France is not typically 'to go.' The French will enjoy their **café** while sitting with friends or just 'people-watching.' **Thé** (tea) is available and can be served **au lait** (with milk), **au citron** (with lemon), **à la menthe** (with mint leaves) or **glacé** (iced). **Tisane** (herbal tea) is also popular.

YOU MAY HEAR...

Voulez-vous boire quelque chose ?
voo • lay • voo bwahr kehl • kuh shohz

Can I get you a drink?

Avec du lait ou du sucre ?
ah • vehk dew lay oo dew sew • kruh

With milk or sugar?

De l'eau gazeuse ou plate ?
duh loh gah • zuhz oo plaht

Sparkling or still water?

APERITIFS, COCKTAILS & LIQUEURS

le cognac   brandy
luh koh • nyahk

le gin   gin
luh zheen

le rhum   rum
luh ruhm

le scotch   scotch
luh skoh • tsh

la tequila   tequila
lah teh • kee • lah

la vodka   vodka
lah vohd • kah

le whisky   whisky
luh wees • kee

Apéritifs are much more common than cocktails. Many
are wine- and brandy-based with herbs and bitters; popular
brands are Amer Picon®, Byrrh®, Dubonnet®, Pernod® and
Ricard®.
Fruit-distilled brandies are popular as after-dinner drinks:
calvados (apple), **kirsch** (cherry), **marc** (grape), poire
William (pear) or quetsche (plum). Other popular liqueurs
include the famous orange-flavored Grand Marnier® and
Cointreau®.

BEER

la bière... *lah beeyehr...*	...beer
en bouteille/pression *awN boo•tehy/preh•seeyohN*	bottled/draft
brune/blonde *brewn/blohNd*	dark/light
blonde/pils *blohNd/peels*	lager/pilsener
locale/importée *loh•kahl/ehN•pohr•tay*	local/imported
non-alcoolisée *noh•nahl•koo•lee•zay*	non-alcoholic

WINE

le vin... *luh vehN...*	...wine
rouge/blanc *roozh/blawN*	red/white
de maison/de table *duh may•zohN/duh tah•bluh*	house/table

sec/sucré	dry/sweet
sehk/sew • kray	
pétillant	sparkling
pay • tee • yawN	
le champagne	champagne
luh shawN • pah • nyuh	
le vin de dessert	dessert wine
luh vehN duh day • sehr	

French wine is world-renowned. In restaurants, a **sommelier** (wine waiter) can offer advice on wine selections that will pair well with your meal—a tip is appreciated for this service.

Region	Main grape varieties	Popular wine
Alsace	Riesling, Pinot Blanc, Gewürztraminer	dry, semi-dry and sweet white wines
Bordeaux	Merlot, Cabernet-Sauvignon, Sémillon, Sauternes	full- and medium-bodied dry red wine; white dessert wine
Burgundy	Pinot Noir, Gamay, Chardonnay	full- and medium-bodied dry red wine; full-bodied dry white wine
Champagne	Chardonnay, Pinot Meunier, Pinot Noir	sparkling wine ranging from sweet to very dry
Côtes du Rhône	Grenache, Syrah, Viognier, Clairette	diverse red wine, from fruity to robust; full-bodied dry white wine

Region	Main grape varieties	Popular wine
Languedoc-Roussillon	Carignan, Grenache, Mourvèdre, Cinsault, Merlot, Syrah	fine and table red wine; semi-dry and dry rosé wine; sweet white wine
Loire	Chenin Blanc, Sauvignon, Muscadet	lighter, dry and semi-dry white wine; some rosé and fruity red wine
Provence	Cinsault, Grenache, Mourvèdre, Syrah	dry and fruity rosé wine; full-bodied dry red wine; some white wine
Corsica	Nieluccio, Sciacarello, Vermentino	dry rosé and red wine; light, dry white wine
Southwest France	Cabernet, Merlot, Sémillon, Sauvignon	full-bodied dry red wine; flavorful white wine

ON THE MENU

les abats
lay zah • bah
organ meat [offal]

les abattis
lay zah • bah • tee
giblets

l'abricot
lah • bree • koh
apricot

l'agneau
lah • nyoh
lamb

l'ail
lie
garlic

l'amande
lah • mawNd
almond

l'ananas
lah • nah • nah
pineapple

l'anchois
lawN • shwah
anchovy

l'andouillette
lawN • doo • yett
French sausage

l'aneth
lah • neht
dill

l'anguille
lawN • gheeyuh
eel

l'artichaut
lahr • tee • shoh
artichoke

l'asperge
lah • spehrzh
asparagus

l'aubergine
loh • buhr • zheen
eggplant [aubergine]

l'avocat
lah • voh • kah
avocado

le babeurre
luh bah • buhr
buttermilk

le bacon
luh beh • kohN

bacon

la banane
lah bah • nahn

banana

le bar
luh bahr

sea bass

le basilic
luh bah • see • leek

basil

la baudroie
lah boh • drwah

monkfish

le beignet
luh beh • nyay

fritter

la betterave
lah beh • tuh • rahv

beet

le beurre
luh buhr

butter

la bière
lah beeyehr

beer

le bifteck d'aloyau
luh beef • tehk dah • lwah • yoh

sirloin

le biscuit
luh bees • kwee

cookie [biscuit]

le blé
luh blay

wheat

le bleu
luh bluh

blue cheese

le bœuf
luh buhf

beef

les bonbons
lay bohN • bohN

candy [sweets]

le boudin
luh boo • dehN

blood sausage

le bouillon
luh boo • yohN

broth

le cabillaud haddock
luh kah • beeyoh

la cacahuète peanut
lah kah • kah • weht

le café coffee
luh kah • fay

la caille quail
lah kie

le calmar squid
luh kahl • mahr

le canard duck
luh kah • nahr

la canneberge cranberry
lah kah • nuh • behrzh

la cannelle cinnamon
lah kah • nehl

la câpre caper
lah kah • pruh

le caramel caramel
luh kah • rah • mehl

la carotte carrot
lah kah • roht

le cassis black currant
luh kah • sees

le céleri celery
luh say • luh • ree

les céréales cereal
lay say • ray • ahl

la cerise cherry
lah suh • reez

la chair de crabe crabmeat
lah shehr duh krahb

le champignon mushroom
luh shawN • pee • nyohN

la charcuterie
lah shar • kew • tuh • ree

cold cuts

la chèvre
lah sheh • vruh

goat

le chevreau
luh shuh • vroh

kid (young goat)

la chicorée
lah shee • koh • ray

chicory

les chips
lay sheeps

potato chips [crisps]

le chocolat
luh shoh • koh • lah

chocolate

le chou
luh shoo

cabbage

le chou rouge
luh shoo roozh

red cabbage

le chou-fleur
luh shoo • fluhr

cauliflower

les choux de Bruxelles
lay shoo duh brewk • sehl

Brussels sprouts

la ciboule
lah see • bool

scallion [spring onion]

le cidre
luh see • druh

cider

le citron
luh see • trohN
lemon

le citron vert
luh see • trohN vehr
lime

la citrouille
lah see • truhy
pumpkin

les cives
lay seev
chives

le clou de girofle
luh kloo duh zhee • roh • fluh
clove

le cœur
luh kuhr
heart

le cognac
luh koh • nyahk
brandy

le colin
luh koh • lehN
hake

la compote
lah kohN • poht
stewed fruit

le concombre
luh kohN • kohN • bruh
cucumber

la confiture
lah kohN • fee • tewr
jam

les coquillages
lay koh • kee • yahzh
shellfish

les coquilles
lay koh • keeyuh
scallops

la coriandre
lah koh • reeyawN • druh
cilantro [coriander]

le cornichon
luh kohr • nee • shohN
gherkin/pickle

la côtelette
lah koh • teh • leht
chop

la courgette
lah koor • zheht
zucchini [courgette]

le crabe   crab
luh krahb

la crème   cream
lah krehm

la crème aigre   sour cream
lah krehm eh • gruh

la crème anglaise   custard
lah krehm awN • glehz

la crème fouettée   cream, whipped
lah krehm fooweh • tay

la crème fraîche   heavy cream
lah krehm frehsh

la crêpe   pancake
lah krehp

le cresson   watercress
luh kruh • sohN

la crevette   shrimp/prawn
lah kruh • veht

le croissant   croissant
luh krwah • sawN

le cumin   cumin
luh kew • mehN

le cumin de près   caraway
luh kew • mehN duh preh

la datte   date
lah daht

la dinde   turkey
lah dehNd

la dorade   sea bass
lah doh • rahd

l'eau   water
loh

l'eau tonique   tonic water
loh toh • neek

l'échalote
lay • shah • loht
shallot

l'edulcorant
lay • dewl • koh • rawN
artificial sweetener

l'endive
lawN • deev
endive

l'épaule
lay • pohl
shoulder

les épices
lay zay • pees
spices

les épinards
lay zay • pee • nahr
spinach

l'escalope (de poulet)
lehs • kah • lohp (duh poo • lay)
breast (of chicken)

l'escargot
lehs • kahr • goh
snail

l'écrevisse
lay • kruh • vees
crayfish

l'espadon
lehs • pah • dohN
swordfish

l'estragon
lehs • trah • gohN
tarragon

le faisan
luh feh • zawN
pheasant

le fenouil
luh fuh • noohy
fennel

la feuille de laurier
lah fuhy duh loh • reeyay
bay leaf

la figue
lah feeg
fig

le filet
luh fee • lay
loin

les fines herbes
lay feen zayrb
herbs

les flageolets
lay flah • zheh • lay

bean sprouts

le flétan
luh flay • tawN

halibut

le foie
luh fwah

liver

la fraise
lah frehz

strawberry

la framboise
lah frawN • bwahz

raspberry

les frites
lay freet

French fries

le fromage
luh froh • mahzh

cheese

le fromage blanc
luh froh • mahzh blawN

soft, creamy cheese

le fromage de chèvre
luh froh • mahzh duh sheh • vruh

goat cheese

le fromage frais
luh froh • mahzh fray

soft, new cheese

le fruit
luh frwee

fruit

les fruits de mer
lay frwee duh mehr

seafood

le gâteau
luh gah • toh

cake

le gâteau sec
luh gah • toh sehk

cracker

la gaufre
lah goh • fruh

waffle

la geléelah
zhuh • lay

jelly

le gibier
luh zhee • beeyay

game

le gigot   leg
luh zhee • goh

le gin   gin
luh zheen

le gingembre   ginger
luh zhehN • zhawN • bruh

la glace   ice cream
lah glahs

le glaçon   ice (cube)
luh glah • sohN

les gombos   okra
lay gohN • boh

le goûter   snack
luh goo • tay

la goyave   guava
lah goh • yahv

la grenade   pomegranate
lah gruh • nahd

la groseille   red currant
lah groh • zehy

le hamburger   hamburger
luh awN • bewr • gayr

le hareng   herring
luh ah • rawN

les haricots   beans
lay ah • ree • koh

les haricots verts   green beans
lay ah • ree • koh vehr

le homard   lobster
luh oh • mahr

le hot dog   hot dog
luh oht dohg

l'huile d'olive   olive oil
lweel doh • leev

l'huître
lwee • truh
oyster

le jambon
luh zhawN • bohN
ham

le jaune/blanc d'œuf
luh zhohn/blawN duhf
egg yolk/white

le jus
luh zhew
juice

le ketchup
luh keht • shuhp
ketchup

le kiwi
luh kee • wee
kiwi

le lait
luh lay
milk

le lait de soja
luh lait duh soh • zhah
soya milk

la laitue
lah lay • tew
lettuce

la langue
lah lawNg
tongue

le lapin
luh lah • pehN
rabbit

les légumes
lay lay • gewm
vegetables

les lentilles
lay lawN • tee • yuh
lentils

la limonade
lah lee • moh • nahd
lemon soda

la liqueur d'oranges
lah lee • kuhr doh • rawNzh
orange liqueur

la liqueur
lah lee • kuhr
liqueur

les macaronis
lay mah • kah • roh • nee
macaroni

le maïs
luh mah • ees

sweet corn

la mandarine
lah mawN • dah • reen

tangerine

la mangue
lah mawNg

mango

le maquereau
luh mah • kuh • roh

mackerel

la margarine
lah mahr • gah • reen

margarine

la marmelade
lah mahr • muh • lahd

marmalade

le marron
luh mah • rohN

chestnut

la mayonnaise
lah mah • yohN • nehz

mayonnaise

le melon
luh muh • lohN

melon

la menthe
lah mawNt

mint

la meringue
lah muh • rehNg

meringue

le miel
luh meeyehl

honey

la morue
lah moh • rew

cod

les moules
lay mool

mussels

la moutarde
lah moo • tahrd

mustard

le mouton
luh moo • tohN

mutton

la mûre
lah mewr

blackberry

la myrtille	blueberry
lah meer•teeyuh	
le navet	turnip
luh nah•vay	
la noisette	hazelnut
lah nwah•zeht	
les noix	nuts
lay nwah	
la noix de cajou	cashew
lah nwah duh kah•zhoo	
la noix de coco	coconut
lah nwah duh koh•koh	
la noix de muscade	nutmeg
lah nwah duh mew•skahd	
la noix de pecan	pecan
lah nwah duh peh•kawN	
la nouille	noodle
lah noohy	
l'œuf	egg
luhf	
l'oie	goose
lwah	
l'oignon	onion
loh•neeyohN	
l'olive	olive
loh•leev	
l'omelette	omelet
loh•muh•leht	
l'orange	orange
loh•rawNzh	
l'orangeade	orange soda
loh•rawN•zhad	[squash]
l'origan	oregano
loh•ree•gawN	

le pain   bread
luh pehN

le pain grillé   toast
luh pehN gree • yay

les palourdes   clams
lay pah • loord

le pamplemousse   grapefruit
luh pawN • pluh • moos

le panais   parsnip
luh pah • nay

la papaye   papaya
lah pah • pie

la pastèque   watermelon
lah pahs • tehk

la patate douce   sweet potato
lah pah • taht doos

la pâte d'amande   marzipan
lah paht dah • mawNd

le pâté   pâté
luh pah • tay

les pâtes   pasta
lay paht

les pâtisseries   pastries
lay pah • tee • suh • ree

la pêche   peach
lah pehsh

la perche   sea perch
lah pehrsh

le persil   parsley
luh pehr • seel

le petit pain   roll
luh puh • tee pehN

les petits pois   peas
lay puh • tee pwah

la pintade
lah pehN•tahd

guinea fowl

la pizza
lah peed•zah

pizza

les pois chiches
lay pwah sheesh

chickpeas

la poire
lah pwahr

pear

le poireau
luh pwah•roh

leek

le poisson
luh pwah•sohN

fish

le poivre
luh pwah•vruh

black pepper

le piment
luh pee•mawN

chili pepper

le poivron
luh pwah•vrohN

pepper (vegetable)

le piment doux
luh pee•mawN doo

sweet pepper

la pomme
lah pohm

apple

la pomme de terre
lah pohm duh tehr

potato

le porc
luh pohr

pork

le porto
luh pohr•toh

port

le potage
luh poh•tahzh

stew

la poule
lah pool

hen

le poulet
luh poo•lay

chicken

le poulpe *luh poolp*	octopus
la prune *lah prewn*	plum
le pruneau *luh prew • noh*	prune
la queue de bœuf *lah kuh duh buhf*	oxtail
le radis *luh rah • dee*	radish
le raisin *luh reh • zehN*	grape
le raisin sec *luh reh • zehN sehk*	raisin
la rhubarbe *lah rew • bahrb*	rhubarb
le rhum *luh ruhm*	rum
le riz *luh ree*	rice
le rognon *luh roh • nyohN*	kidney
le romarin *luh roh • mah • rehN*	rosemary

le rôti
luh roh • tee
roast

le rôti de bœuf
luh roh • tee duh buhf
roast beef

le safran
luh sah • frawN
saffron

la salade
lah sah • lahd
salad

le sandwich
luh sawN • dweesh
sandwich

la sardine
lah sahr • deen
sardine

la sauce
lah sohs
sauce

la sauce à l'ail
lah sohs ah lie
garlic sauce

la sauce aigre douce
lah sohs eh • gruh doos
sweet and sour sauce

la sauce piquante
lah sohs pee • kawNt
hot pepper sauce

la sauce soja
lah sohs soh • zhah
soy sauce

la saucisse
lah soh • sees
sausage

le saucisson
luh soh • see • sohN
salami

la sauge
lah sohzh
sage

le saumon
luh soh • mohN
salmon

la scarole
lah skah • rohl
escarole [chicory]

le scotch
luh skoh • tsh
scotch

le sel	salt
luh sehl	
le sherry	sherry
luh sheh • ree	
le sirop	syrup
luh see • roh	
le soda	soda
luh soh • dah	
le soja	soy [soya]/soybean
luh soh • zhah	[soya bean]
la sole	sole
lah sohl	
la soupe	soup
lah soop	
les spaghettis	spaghetti
lay spah • geh • tee	
les spiritueux	spirits
lay spee • ree • tewuh	
le steak	steak
luh stayk	
le sucre	sugar
luh sew • kruh	
les sucreries	sweets
lay sew • kreh • ree	
la tarte	pie
lah tahrt	
le thé	tea
luh tay	
le thon	tuna
luh tohN	
le thym	thyme
luh tehN	
le tofu	tofu
luh toh • few	

la tomate　　　　　　　tomato
lah toh • maht

les tripes　　　　　　　tripe
lay treep

la truffe　　　　　　　truffle
lah trewf

la truite　　　　　　　trout
lah trweet

la vanille　　　　　　　vanilla
lah vah • neeyuh

le veau　　　　　　　veal
luh voh

la venaison　　　　　　venison
lah vuh • neh • sohN

le vermouth　　　　　　vermouth
luh vehr • moot

la viande　　　　　　　meat
lah veeyawNd

le vin　　　　　　　wine
luh vehN

le vin de dessert　　　　dessert wine
luh vehN duh day • sehr

le vinaigre　　　　　　vinegar
luh vee • neh • gruh

la vodka　　　　　　　vodka
lah vohd • kah

la volaille　　　　　　poultry
lah voh • lie

le whisky　　　　　　whisky
luh wees • kee

le yaourt　　　　　　yogurt
luh yah • oort

PEOPLE

GOING OUT   **224**

ROMANCE   **228**

GOING OUT

NEED TO KNOW

What's there to do at night?	**Que peut-on faire le soir ?**
	kuh puh • tohN fehr luh swahr
Do you have a program of events?	**Avez-vous un programme des festivités ?**
	ah • vay • voo uhN proh • grahm day fehs • tee • vee • tay
What's playing tonight?	**Qui joue ce soir ?**
	kee zhoo suh swahr
Where's...?	**Où est...?**
	oo ay...
the downtown area	**le centre ville**
	luh sawN • truh veel
the bar	**le bar**
	luh bahr
the dance club	**la discothèque**
	lah dees • koh • tehk

ENTERTAINMENT

Can you recommend…?	**Pouvez-vous me conseiller…?**
	poo•vay•voo muh kohN•say•yay…
a concert	**un concert**
	uhN kohN•sehr
a movie	**un film**
	uhN feelm
an opera	**un opéra**
	uhN noh•pay•rah
a play	**une pièce de théâtre**
	ewn peeyehs duh tay•ah•truh
When does it start/end?	**Quand est-ce que ça commence/finit ?**
	kawN tehs kuh sah koh•mawNs/fee•nee
What's the dress code?	**Quelle est la tenue exigée ?**
	kehl ay lah tuh•new ehk•see•zhay
I like…	**J'aime…**
	zhehm…
classical music	**la musique classique**
	lah mew•zeek klah•seek
folk music	**la musique folklorique**
	lah mew•zeek fohl•kloh•reek
jazz	**le jazz**
	luh zhahz
pop music	**la pop musique**
	lah pohp mew•zeek
rap	**le rap**
	luh rahp

For Tickets, see page 20.

Tourist information offices can provide information on local entertainment. Newspapers will usually list upcoming events. In the larger cities, there are magazines and publications that list the bars, clubs and other venues and activities of interest. These magazines can usually be found in bookstores or newsstands. Your hotel concierge can also help you find entertainment options.

NIGHTLIFE

What's there to do at night?	**Que peut-on faire le soir ?**
	kuh puh • tohN fehr luh swahr
Can you recommend…?	**Pouvez-vous me conseiller…?**
	poo • vay • voo muh kohN • say • yay…
a bar	**un bar**
	uhN bahr
a cabaret	**un cabaret**
	uhN kah • bah • ray
a casino	**un casino**
	uhN kah • zee • noh

a dance club	**une discothèque** *ewn dees • koh • tehk*
a gay club	**un club gay** *uhN kluhb gay*
a jazz club	**un club de jazz** *uhN kluhb duh zhahz*
a club with French music	**un club de musique française** *uhN kluhb duh mew • zeek frawN • sehz*
Is there live music?	**Y-a-t-il des concerts?** *yah • teel day kohN • sehr*
How do I get there?	**Comment est-ce que je m'y rends ?** *koh • mawN tehs kuh zhuh mee rawN*
Is there a cover charge?	**Y-a-t-il un droit d'entrée ?** *yah • teel uhN drwah dawN • tray*
Let's go dancing.	**Allons danser.** *ah • lohN dawN • say*
Is this area safe at night?	**Est-ce que cet endroit est sûr la nuit ?** *ehs kuh seht awN • drwah ay sewr lah nwee*

YOU MAY HEAR...

Éteignez vos portables, s'il vous plaît.
ay • teh • nyay voh pohr • tah • bluh seel voo play

Turn off
your mobile
phones, please.

ROMANCE

NEED TO KNOW

Would you like to go out for a drink/dinner?	**Voudriez-vous aller prendre un verre/sortir dîner ?** *voo•dreeyay•voo ah•lay prawN•druh uhN vehr/sohr•teer dee•nay*
What are your plans for tonight/tomorrow?	**Quels sont vos projets pour ce soir/demain ?** *kehl sohN voh proh•zhay poor suh swahr/duh•mehN*
Can I have your (phone) number?	**Puis-je avoir votre numéro (de téléphone) ?** *pwee•zhuh ah•vwahr voh•truh new•may•roh (duh tay•lay•fohn)*
Can I join you?	**Puis-je me joindre à vous ?** *pwee•zhuh muh zhwehN•druh ah voo*
Can I buy you a drink?	**Puis-je vous offrir un verre ?** *pwee•zhuh voo zoh•freer uhN vehr*
I love you.	**Je t'aime.** *zhuh tehm*

THE DATING GAME

Would you like to go out...?	**Voudriez-vous sortir...?** *voo•dreeyay•voo sohr•teer...*
for coffee	**prendre un café** *prawN•druh uhN kah•fay*

for a drink	**prendre un verre**
	prawN • druh uhN vehr
to dinner	**aller dîner**
	ah • lay dee • nay
What are your plans for…?	**Quels sont vos projets pour…?**
	kehl sohN voh proh • zhay poor…
today	**aujourd'hui**
	oh • zhoor • dwee
tonight	**ce soir**
	suh swahr
tomorrow	**demain**
	duh • mehN
this weekend	**ce weekend**
	suh wee • kehnd
Where would you like to go?	**Où voudriez-vous aller ?**
	oo voo • dreeay • voo ah • lay
I'd like to go to…	**Je voudrais aller à…**
	zhuh voo • dray ah • lay ah…
Do you like…?	**Aimez-vous…?**
	eh • may • voo…
Can I have your phone number/ e-mail ?	**Puis-je avoir votre numero de téléphone/mail ?**
	pwee • zhuh ah • vwahr voh • truh new • may • roh duh tay • lay • fohn/mehyl
Are you on Facebook /Twitter?	**Êtes-vous sur Facebook/Twitter ?**
	eht • voo sewr fayhs • book/twee • teuhr
Can I join you?	**Puis-je me joindre à vous ?**
	pwee • zhuh muh zhwehN • druh ah voo
You're very attractive.	**Vous êtes très beau** *m*/**belle** *f*.
	voo zeht tray boh/behl
Let's go somewhere quieter.	**Allons dans un endroit plus calme.**
	ah • lohN dawN zuhN nawN • drwah plew kahlm

For Communications, see page 84.

ACCEPTING & REJECTING

I'd love to.	**Avec plaisir.**
	ah • vehk play • zeer
Where should we meet?	**Où devons-nous nous retrouver ?**
	oo duh • vohN • noo noo ruh • troo • vay
I'll meet you at the bar/your hotel.	**Je vous retrouverai au bar/à votre hôtel.**
	zhuh voo ruh • troo • vuh • ray oh bahr/ah voh • truh oh • tehl
I'll come by at…	**Je viendrai à…**
	zhuh veeyehN • dray ah…
I'm busy.	**Je suis occupé** *m*/**occupée** *f.*
	zhuh swee zoh • kew • pay
I'm not interested.	**Je ne suis pas intéressé** *m*/**intéressée** *f.*
	zhuh nuh swee pah ehN • tay • reh • say
Leave me alone.	**Laissez-moi tranquille.**
	leh • say mwah trawN • keel
Stop bothering me!	**Fichez-moi la paix !**
	fee • shay • mwah lah pay

GETTING INTIMATE

Can I hug/kiss you?	**Puis-je vous enlacer/embrasser ?**
	pwee • zhuh voo zawN • lah • say/ zawN • brah • say
Yes.	**Oui.**
	wee
No.	**Non.**
	nohN
Stop!	**Arrêtez !**
	ah • reh • tay
I love you.	**Je t'aime.**
	zhuh tehm

SEXUAL PREFERENCES

Are you gay?	**Êtes-vous gay ?**
	eht • voo gay
I'm…	**Je suis…**
	zhuh swee…
heterosexual	**hétérosexuel** *m*/**hétérosexuelle** *f*
	ay • tay • roh • sehk • sewehl
homosexual	**homosexuel** *m*/**homosexuelle** *f*
	oh • moh • sehk • sewehl
bisexual	**bisexuel** *m*/**bisexuelle** *f*
	bee • sehk • sewehl
Do you like men/women?	**Aimez-vous les hommes/femmes ?**
	ay • may • voo lay zohm/fahm

DICTIONARY

ENGLISH–FRENCH
234

FRENCH–ENGLISH
258

ENGLISH–FRENCH

A

abbey l'abbaye
accept v accepter
access v accéder; n accés
accident l'accident
accommodation le logement
account le compte
acetaminophen le
  paracétamol
acupuncture l'acuponcture
adapter l'adaptateur
address l'adresse
admission l'entrée
after après; ~noon l'après-
  midi; ~shave l'après-rasage
age l'âge
agency l'agence
AIDS Déficience le Syndrome
  d'immunodéficience acquise
air l'air; ~conditioning la
  climatisation; ~pump la
  pompe à air; ~line la
  compagnie aérienne;
  ~mail par avion;
  ~plane l'avion;
  ~port l'aéroport
aisle (plane) le couloir;

~(theater) l'allée; ~seat le
  siège couloir
allergic allergique;
  ~reaction la réaction
  allergique
allow v permettre
alone seul
alter v modifier
aluminum foil le papier
  aluminium
amazing surprenant
ambulance l'ambulance
American américain
amusement park le parc
  d'attractions
and et
anemic anémique
anesthesia l'anesthésie
animal l'animal
ankle la cheville
antibiotic l'antibiotique
antiques store l'antiquaire
antiseptic cream la crème
  antiseptique
anything rien
apartment l'appartement
appendix (body

| adj adjective | BE British English | v verb |
| adv adverb | n noun | |

part) l'appendice
appetizer l'entrée
appointment le rendez-vous
arcade la salle de jeux
area code le code régional
arm le bras
aromatherapy
l'aromathérapie
around (the corner) au coin
arrivals (airport) les arrivées
arrive v arriver
artery l'artère
arthritis l'arthrite
art l'art
Asian asiatique
aspirin l'aspirine
asthmatic asthmatique
ATM le distributeur
automatique de billets;
~card la carte de retrait
attack l'attaque
attend v participer
attraction (place) le lieu
touristique
attractive beau
Australia l'Australie
Australian australien
automatic automatique;
~car la voiture automatique
available disponible

B

baby le bébé; **~bottle** le
biberon; **~wipe** la lingette
pour bébé; **~sitter** le baby-
sitter
back (body part) le dos;
~ache le mal de dos;
~pack le sac à dos
bag le sac
baggage [BE] le bagage;
~claim le -retrait des
bagages; **~ticket** l'étiquette
bakery la boulangerie
ballet le ballet
bandage le pansement
bank la banque
bar (place) le bar
barbecue le barbecue
barber le coiffeur pour
hommes
baseball le baseball
basket (grocery store) le
panier
basketball le basketball
bathroom la salle de bains
battery la pile
battleground le champ de
bataille
be v être
beach la plage
beautiful beau
bed le lit; **~and breakfast**
le bed and breakfast
before avant
begin v commencer
beginner le débutant
behind derrière
beige beige
belt la ceinture

berth la couchette

best meilleur

better mieux

bicycle la bicyclette; le vélo

big grand ~**bigger** plus grand

bike route la piste cyclable

bikini le bikini; ~**wax** l'épilation à la cire du maillot

bill (charge) v facturer; ~n **(invoice)** la facture; ~n **(money)** la coupure; ~n **(of sale)** le reçu

bird l'oiseau

birthday l'anniversaire

black noir

bladder la vessie

bland sans goût

blanket la couverture

bleed v saigner

blood le sang; ~**pressure** la tension

blouse le chemisier

blue bleu

board v embarquer; ~**ing pass** la carte d'embarquement

boat le bateau

bone l'os

book le livre; ~**store** la librairie

boots les bottes

boring ennuyant

botanical garden le jardin botanique

bother v ennuyer

bottle la bouteille; ~**opener** l'ouvre-bouteille

bowl le saladier

box la boîte

boxing match le match de boxe

boy le garçon; ~**friend** le petit-ami

bra le soutien-gorge

bracelet le bracelet

brakes (car) les freins

break v **(tooth/bone)** casser

breakdown la panne

breakfast le petit déjeuner

break-in (burglary) l'effraction

breast le sein; ~**feed** v allaiter

breathe v respirer

bridge pont

briefs (clothing) les slips

bring v apporter

British anglais

broken cassé

brooch la broche

broom le balai

brother le frère

brown marron

bug l'insecte

building le bâtiment

burn v brûler

bus le bus; ~**station** la gare routière; ~**stop** l'arrêt de bus; ~**ticket** le ticket de bus; ~**tour** la visite en bus

business les affaires;
~**card** la carte de visite;
~**center** le centre d'affaires;
~**class** la classe affaire;
~**hours** les heures
d'ouverture
butcher le boucher
buttocks les fesses
buy *v* acheter
bye au revoir

C

cabaret le cabaret
cabin la cabine
cable car le téléphérique
café le café
call *v* appeler;
~**collect** appeler ~ *n* l'appel
en PCV;
calories les kilocalories
camera l'appareil photo;
~**case** le sac à appareil
photo; ~**store** la boutique
photo
camp *v* camper; ~**ing**
stove le réchaud; ~**site** le
camping
can opener le l'ouvre-boîte
Canada le Canada
Canadian canadien
cancel *v* annuler
candy le bonbon
canned goods les conserves
canyon la gorge
car la voiture; ~**hire** [BE] la
voiture de location; ~**park**
[BE] le parking; **rental** ~ la
voiture de location; ~**seat** le
siège bébé
carafe la carafe
card la carte; **ATM** ~ la carte
de retrait; **credit** ~ la carte
de crédit; **phone** ~ le carte
de téléphone
carry-on (piece of hand
luggage) le bagage à main
cart le chariot
carton le paquet; ~**of**
cigarettes la cartouche de
cigarettes
case (amount) le cas
cash *v* encaisser; ~ *n* le
liquide; ~**advance** l'avance
cashier la caisse
casino le casino
castle le château
cathedral la cathédrale
cave la grotte
CD le CD (disque compact)
cell phone le portable
Celsius Celsius
centimeter le centimètre
certificate le certificat
chair la chaise; ~**lift** le
télésiège
change *v* (baby) changer;
~**(money)** échanger; ~*n*
(money) la monnaie;
charcoal le charbon de bois
charge *v* **(credit card)** payer

par carte

charge (cost) le coût

cheap bon marché

cheaper moins cher

check v **(luggage)** enregistrer; ~**(on something)** vérifier; ~n **(payment)** le chèque; ~**-in (hotel/ airport)** l'enregistrement; ~**ing account** le compte courant; ~**-out (hotel)** quitter la chambre

Cheers! Santé!

chemical toilet les toilettes portables

chemist [BE] la pharmacie

cheque [BE] le chèque

chest (body part) la poitrine; ~**pain** la douleur à la poitrine

chewing gum le chewing-gum

child l'enfant; ~'**s seat** le siège enfant

children's menu le menu enfant

children's portion la portion enfant

chopsticks les baguettes

church l'église

cigar le cigare

cigarette la cigarette

class la classe

classical music la musique classique

clean v nettoyer; ~ adj propre; ~**ing product** le produit d'entretien; ~**ing supplies** les produits d'entretien

clear v **(on an ATM)** effacer

cliff la falaise

cling film [BE] le cellophane

close v **(shop)** fermer; ~ adv près; ~**d** fermé

clothing les vêtements; ~**store** le magasin de vêtements

club le club

coat le manteau

coffee shop le café

coin la pièce

colander la passoire

cold (sickness) le rhume; ~**(temperature)** froid

colleague le collègue

cologne l'eau de Cologne

color la couleur

comb le peigne

come v venir

complaint la plainte

computer l'ordinateur

concert le concert; ~**hall** la salle de concert

condition (medical) l'état de santé

conditioner l'après-shampooing

condom le préservatif

conference la conférence

confirm v confirmer

congestion la congestion

connect *v* (internet) se
connecter

connection (flight) la
correspondance;
~(internet) la connexion

constipated constipé

consulate le consulat

consultant le consultant

contact *v* contacter

contact lens les lentilles
de contact; ~solution la
solution pour lentilles de
contact

contagious contagieux

convention hall le palais des
congrès

conveyor belt le carrousel

cook *v* cuisiner; ~ing gas le
gaz

cool (temperature) frais

copper le cuivre

corkscrew le tire-bouchon

cost *v* coûter

cot le lit pliant

cotton le coton

cough *v* tousser; ~ *n* la toux

country code le code national

cover charge (bar,
club) le droit d'entrée;
~(restaurant) le couvert

crash *v* (car) avoir un
accident

cream (ointment) la crème

credit card la carte de crédit

crew neck le col rond

crib le berceau

crystal le cristal

cup la tasse

currency la monnaie;
~exchange l'échange
de monnaie; ~exchange
office le bureau de change

current account [BE] le
compte courant

customs la douane

cut *v* couper; ~ *n* (injury) la
coupure

cute mignon

cycling faire du vélo

D

damage *v* abîmer;
~d endommagé

dance *v* danser; ~club la
discothèque; ~ing dansant

dangerous dangereux

dark sombre

date (calendar) la date

day le jour

deaf sourd

debit card la carte de retrait

deck chair la chaise longue

declare *v* déclarer

decline *v* (credit card) refuser

deeply profondément

degree (temperature) le
degré

delay *v* retarder

delete *v* (computer)
supprimer

delicatessen la charcuterie

delicious délicieux

denim jean

dentist le dentiste

denture le dentier

deodorant le déodorant

department store le grand magasin

departures (airport) les départs

deposit v déposer; ~**(bank)** le dépôt

desert le désert

detergent le détergent

develop v **(film)** développer

diabetic diabétique

dial v composer

diamond le diamant

diaper la couche

diarrhea la diarrhée

diesel le gazole

difficult difficile

digital numérique; ~**camera** l'appareil photo numérique; ~**photo** la photo numérique

dining room la salle à manger

dinner le dîner

direction la direction

dirty sale

disabled [BE] handicapé; ~**accessible [BE]** accessible aux handicapés

disconnect v **(computer)** déconnecter

discount la réduction

dish (kitchen) la vaisselle; ~**washer** le lave-vaisselle; ~**washing liquid** le détergent pour lave-vaisselle

display montrer; ~**case** la vitrine

disposable jetable; ~**razor** le rasoir jetable

dive v plonger; ~**ing equipment** l'équipement de plongée

divorce v divorcer

dizzy avoir des vertiges

doctor le docteur

doll la poupée

dollar (U.S.) le dollar

domestic national; ~**flight** le vol national

door la porte

dormitory le dortoir

double bed le lit double

downtown (direction) vers le centre-ville; ~**area** le centre-ville

dozen la douzaine

drag lift le remonte-pentes

dress (piece of clothing) la robe; ~**code** la tenue exigée

drink v boire; ~ n la boisson; ~**menu** la carte des boissons

drinking water l'eau potable

drive v conduire; ~**r's license number** le numéro de

permis de conduire
drop (medicine) la goutte
drowsiness la somnolence
dry cleaner la teinturerie
dubbed doublé
during pendant
duty (tax) la taxe
duty-free hors taxe
DVD DVD

E

ear l'oreille; ~**ache** l'otite
early tôt
earrings les boucles d'oreille
east est
easy facile
eat v manger
economy class la classe
économique
elbow le coude
electric outlet la prise
électrique
elevator l'ascenseur
e-mail v envoyer un mail;
~n le mail; ~address
l'adresse mail
emergency l'urgence; ~exit
la sortie de secours
empty v vider
enamel (jewelry) l'émail
end v finir
English anglais
engrave v graver
enjoy v prendre plaisir
enter v entrer

entertainment le
divertissement
entrance l'entrée
envelope l'enveloppe
equipment l'équipement
escalators l'escalator
e-ticket le billet électronique
EU resident le résident
européen
euro l'euro
evening la soirée
excess l'excès
exchange v échanger; ~n
(place) le bureau de change;
~**rate** le taux de change
excursion l'excursion
excuse v excuser
exhausted épuisé
exit v sortir; ~n la sortie
expensive cher
expert (skill level) l'expert
exposure (film) la pose
express express; ~**bus**
le bus direct; ~**train**
l'express
extension (phone) le poste
extra extra; ~**large** très grand
extract v **(tooth)** arracher
eye l'œil
eyebrow wax l'épilation à la
cire des sourcils

F

face le visage
facial le soin du visage

family la famille
fan (appliance) le ventilateur;
~**(souvenir)** l'éventail
far loin
farm la ferme
far-sighted presbyte
fast vite; ~**food** le fast food
faster plus vite
fat free 0% de matières
grasses
father le père
fax v envoyer un fax; ~n le fax;
~**number** le numéro de fax
feed v nourrir
ferry le ferry
fever la fièvre
field (sports) le terrain de
sport
fill v faire le plein
fill v **out (form)** remplir
filling (tooth) le plombage
film (camera) la pellicule
fine (fee for breaking law) la
contravention
finger le doigt; ~**nail** l'ongle
fire le feu; ~**department** les
pompiers; ~**door** la porte
coupe-feu
first premier; ~**class** la
première classe
fitting room la cabine
d'essayage
fix v **(repair)** réparer
flashlight la lampe torche
flat tire [tyre BE] le pneu

crevé
flight le vol
floor le sol
flower la fleur
folk music la musique
folklorique
food la nourriture
foot le pied
football [BE] le football;
~**game [BE]** le match de
football
for pour
forecast la météo
forest la forêt
fork la fourchette
form le formulaire
formula (baby) le lait pour
bébés
fort le fort
fountain la fontaine
France la France
free libre
freezer le congélateur
French français
fresh frais
friend l'ami
frying pan la poêle
full-service le service complet
full-time le temps plein

G

game le match
garage le garage
garbage bag le sac poubelle
gas l'essence; ~**station** la

station service

gate (airport) la porte

gay gay; **~bar** le bar gay; **~club** le club gay

gel (hair) le gel

get off v **(a train, bus, subway)** descendre

get to v aller

gift le cadeau; **~shop** la boutique cadeaux

girl la fille; **~friend** la petite-amie

give v donner

glass le verre;

glasses les lunettes

go v **(somewhere)** aller

gold l'or

golf course le terrain de golf

golf tournament le tournoi de golf

good adj bon; **~n** le produit; **~afternoon** bon après-midi; **~evening** bonsoir; **~morning** bonjour; **~bye** au revoir

goods les produits

gram le gramme

grandchild les petits-enfants

grandparent les grands-parents

gray gris

green vert

grocery store le magasin de fruits et légumes

ground floor le rez-de-chaussée

groundcloth le tapis de sol

groundsheet le drap du dessous

group le groupe

guide le guide; **~book** le guide; **~dog** le chien d'aveugle

gym la gym

gynecologist le gynécologue

H

hair les cheveux; **dryer** le sèche-cheveux d'étudiant; **~salon** le coiffeur; **~brush** la brosse; **~cut** la coupe de cheveux; **~spray** la laque; **~style** le style de coiffure; **~stylist** le coiffeur

half la moitié; **~hour** la demi-heure; **~-kilo** le demi-kilo

hammer le marteau

hand la main; **~luggage [BE]** le bagage à main; **~bag [BE]** le sac à main

handicapped l'handicapé; **~-accessible** accessible aux handicapés

hangover la gueule de bois

happy heureux

hat le chapeau

have v avoir

head (body part) la tête; **~ache** le mal de tête; **~phones** les écouteurs

health la santé; **~food store** le magasin de produits diététiques
heart le cœur; **~condition** le problème cardiaque
heat le chauffage; **~er** le chauffage
hectare l'hectare
hello bonjour
helmet le casque
help v aider; **~n** l'aide
here ici
hi salut
high haut; **~chair** la chaise haute; **~-heeled shoes** les chaussures à talons aiguilles; **~way** l'autoroute
hiking boots les chaussures de marche
hill la colline
hire v [BE] louer; **~car** [BE] la voiture de location
hitchhike v faire de l'auto-stop
hockey le hockey
holiday [BE] les vacances
horsetrack le champ de course
hospital l'hôpital
hostel l'auberge de jeunesse
hot (spicy) épicé; **~(temperature)** chaud; **~spring** la source chaude; **~water** l'eau chaude
hotel l'hôtel

hour l'heure
house la maison; **~hold goods** les produits ménagers; **~keeping service** le service d'entretien
how comment; **~much** combien
hug v enlacer
hungry faim
hurt la douleur
husband le mari

I

ibuprofen l'ibuprofène
ice la glace; **~hockey** le hockey sur glace
icy glacé
identification l'identification
ill malade
in dans
include v inclure
indoor pool la piscine intérieure
inexpensive pas cher
infected infecté
information (phone) les renseignements; **~desk** le bureau des renseignements
insect l'insecte; **~bite** la piqure d'insecte; **~repellent** la lotion anti-insectes
insert v insérer
insomnia l'insomnie

instant message le message instantané

insulin l'insuline

insurance l'assurance; ~**card** la carte d'assurance; ~**company** la compagnie d'assurance

interesting intéressant

intermediate le niveau intermédiaire

international (airport area) l'international (terminal); ~**flight** le vol international; ~**student card** la carte internationale d'étudiant

internet l'internet; ~**cafe** le cyber café; ~**service** le service internet

interpreter l'interprète

intersection l'intersection

intestine l'intestin

introduce *v* présenter

invoice [BE] la facture

Ireland l'Irlande

Irish irlandais

iron *v* repasser; ~*n* (clothes) le fer à repasser

Italian italien

J

jacket la veste

jar le pot

jaw la mâchoire

jazz le jazz; ~**club** le club de jazz

jeans le jean

jet ski le jet ski

jeweler la bijouterie

jewelry le bijou

join *v* joindre

joint (body part) l'articulation

K

key la clé; ~**card** la carte de la chambre; ~**ring** la chaîne

kiddie pool la pataugeoire

kidney (body part) le rein

kilo le kilo; ~**gram** le kilogramme; ~**meter** le kilomètre

kiss *v* embrasser

kitchen la cuisine; ~**foil** [BE] le papier aluminium

knee le genou

knife le couteau

L

lace la dentelle

lactose intolerant allergique au lactose

lake le lac

large grand

larger plus grand

last dernier

late (time) tard

later plus tard

laundromat la laverie automatique

laundry la lessive; ~**facility** la

buanderie; **~service** le service de nettoyage

lawyer l'avocat

leather le cuir

leave v partir

left (direction) à gauche

leg la jambe

lens le verre

less moins

lesson la leçon

letter la lettre

library la bibliothèque

life jacket le gilet de sauvetage

lifeguard le secouriste

lift [BE] l'ascenseur; **~pass** le forfait

light (cigarette) v allumer; **~adj (overhead)** blond; **~bulb** l'ampoule

lighter le briquet

like v aimer

line (train) la ligne

linen le lin

lip les lèvres

liquor store le marchand de vins et de spiritueux

liter le litre

little adv peu; ~adj petit

live v vivre

liver (body part) le foie

loafers les mocassins

local du quartier

lock v fermer; ~n le cadenas; **~er** la consigne

log off (computer) terminer une session

log on (computer) ouvrir une session

long long; **~sleeves** les manches longues; **~-sighted [BE]** presbyte

look v regarder

lose v **(something)** perdre

lost perdu; **~and found** les objets trouvés

lotion la crème

louder plus fort

love v **(someone)** aimer; ~n amour

low bas

luggage le bagage; **~cart** le chariot; **~locker** la consigne; **~ticket** le retrait des bagages

lunch le déjeuner

lung le poumon

M

magazine le magazine

magnificent magnifique

mail le courrier; **~box** la boîte-à-lettres

main attraction la principale attraction touristique

main course le plat principal

mall le centre commercial

man l'homme

manager le responsable

manicure la manucure

manual car la voiture manuelle
map la carte
market le marché
married marié
marry v se marier
mass (church service) la messe
massage le massage
match le match
meal le repas
measure v **(someone)** mesurer
measuring cup la mesure
measuring spoon la cuillère à doser
mechanic le mécanicien
medicine le médicament
medium (size) moyen
meet v **(someone)** rencontrer
meeting la réunion; **~room** la salle de réunion
membership card la carte de membre
memorial (place) le lieu commémoratif
memory card la carte mémoire
mend v raccourcir
menstrual cramp les règles douloureuses
menu la carte
message le message
meter (parking) l'horodateur
microwave le micro-onde

midday [BE] midi
midnight minuit
mileage le kilométrage
mini-bar le mini bar
minute la minute
missing disparu
mistake l'erreur
mobile home le mobile home
mobile phone [BE] le portable
mobility la mobilité
money l'argent
month le mois
mop la serpillière
moped la mobylette
more plus
morning le matin
mosque la mosquée
mother la mère
motion sickness (air) le mal de l'air; **~(sea)** le mal de mer
motor boat le bateau à moteur
motorcycle la mobylette
motorway [BE] l'autoroute
mountain la montagne
mousse la mousse
mouth la bouche
movie le film; **~theater** le cinéma
mug v attaquer
muscle le muscle
museum le musée
music la musique; **~store** le disquaire

N

nail file la lime á ongle
nail salon l'onglerie
name le nom
napkin la serviette
nappies [BE] les couches
nationality la nationalité
nature preserve la réserve naturelle
nausea la nausée
near près; ~**by** près de; ~~**-sighted** myope
neck le cou
necklace le collier
need v avoir besoin
newspaper le journal
newsstand le kiosque à journaux
next suivant
nice bien
night la nuit
nightclub le night club
no non
non-alcoholic non alcoolisé
non-smoking non fumeur
noon midi
north nord
nose le nez
note [BE] la coupure
nothing rien
notify v informer
novice (skill level) novice
now maintenant
number le nombre; le numéro

nurse l'infirmier

O

office le bureau; ~**hours** les heures d'ouverture
off-licence [BE] le marchand de vins et de spiritueux
oil l'huile
OK d'accord
old vieux
on the corner au coin
once une fois
one un; ~~**-way (ticket)** l'aller simple; ~~**-way street** le sens unique
only seulement
open v ouvrir; ~ adj ouvert
opera l'opéra; ~**house** l'opéra
opposite le contraire
optician l'opticien
orange (color) orange
orchestra l'orchestre
order v commander
outdoor pool la piscine extérieure
outside dehors
over-the-counter (medication) sans ordonnance
overlook (scenic place) le point d'observation
overnight de nuit
oxygen treatment le soin à l'oxygène

P

pacifier la tétine
pack v faire les bagages
package le colis
pad [BE] la serviette hygiénique
pain la douleur
pajamas le pyjama
palace le palais
panties les culottes
pants le pantalon
pantyhose le collant
paper le papier; ~**towel** la serviette en papier
paracetamol [BE] le paracétamol
park v se garer; ~n le parc; ~**ing garage** le garage; ~**ing lot** le parking
part (for car) la pièce; ~**-time** le temps partiel
pass through v passer
passenger le passager
passport le passeport; ~**control** le contrôle de passeport
password le mot de passe
pastry shop la pâtisserie
path le chemin
pay v payer; ~**phone** le téléphone public
peak (of a mountain) le sommet
pearl la perle

pedestrian le piéton
pediatrician le pédiatre
pedicure la pédicure
pen le stylo
penicillin la pénicilline
penis le pénis
per par; ~**day** par jour; ~**hour** par heure; ~**night** par nuit; ~**week** par semaine
perfume le parfum
period (menstrual) les règles; ~**(of time)** la période
permit v permettre
personal identification number (PIN) le code secret
petite menue
petrol [BE] le l'essence; ~**station [BE]** la station service
pewter l'étain
pharmacy la pharmacie
phone v téléphoner; ~n le téléphone; ~**call** l'appel; ~**card** la carte de téléphone; ~**number** le numéro de téléphone
photo la photo; ~**copy** la photocopie; ~**graphy** la photographie
pick up v (something) prendre
picnic area l'aire de pique-nique
piece le morceau
Pill (birth control) la pilule

pillow l'oreiller
pink rose
piste [BE] la piste; **~map [BE]** la carte des pistes
pizzeria la pizzeria
place v **(a bet)** parier
plane l'avion
plastic wrap le cellophane
plate l'assiette
platform le quai
platinum platine
play v jouer; **~n (theater)** la pièce; **~ground** l'aire de jeux; **~pen** le parc
please s'il vous plaît
pleasure le plaisir
plunger le déboucheur de toilettes
plus size grande taille
pocket la poche
poison le poison
poles (skiing) les bâtons
police la police; **~report** le rapport de police; **~station** le commissariat de police
pond l'étang
pool la piscine
pop music la pop musique
portion la portion
post [BE] le courrier; **~office** le bureau de poste; **~box [BE]** la boîte-à-lettres; **~card** la carte postale
pot la casserole

pottery la poterie
pound (British sterling) la livre sterling
pregnant enceinte
prescribe v prescrire
prescription l'ordonnance
press v **(clothing)** repasser
price le prix
print v imprimer
problem le problème
produce v produire; **~store** le marchand de fruits et légumes
prohibit v interdire
pronounce v prononcer
public public
pull v **(door sign)** tirer
purple pourpre
purse le sac
push v **(door sign)** pousser
pushchair [BE] la poussette

Q

quality la qualité
question la question
quiet le silence; le calme

R

racetrack la piste de courses
racket (sports) la raquette
railway station [BE] la gare
rain la pluie; **~coat** l'imperméable; **~forest** la forêt vierge
rainy pluvieux

rap (music) le rap

rape v violer; **~n** le viol

rash l'irritation cutanée

razor blade la lame de rasoir

reach v atteindre

ready prêt

real vrai

receipt le reçu

receive v recevoir

reception la réception

recharge v recharger

recommend v recommander

recommendation la recommandation

recycling les ordures à recycler

red rouge

refrigerator le réfrigérateur

region la région

registered mail le courrier recommandé

regular ordinaire

relationship la relation

rent v louer; **~al car** la voiture de location

repair v réparer

repeat v répéter

reservation la réservation; **~desk** le bureau de réservation

reserve v réserver

restaurant le restaurant

restroom les toilettes

retired v prendre sa retraite

return v (something) rendre;

~n [BE] l'aller-retour

rib (body part) la côte

right (direction) à droite; **~of way** le droit de passage

ring la bague

river la rivière

road map la carte routière

rob v voler

romantic romantique

room la pièce; **~key** la clé; **~service** le service de chambre

round-trip l'aller-retour

route la route

rowboat la barque

rubbish [BE] les poubelles; **~bag [BE]** le sac poubelle

rugby le rugby

ruins les ruines

S

sad triste

safe adj en sécurité; **~n** le coffre-fort

sales tax la TVA

same le même

sandals les sandales

sanitary napkin la serviette hygiénique

saucepan la casserole

sauna le sauna

save v (computer) sauvegarder

savings (account) le compte épargne

scanner scanner
scarf l'écharpe
schedule v prévoir; ~n l'horaire
science la science
scissors les ciseaux
sea la mer
seat le siège
security la sécurité
see v voir
self-service le self-service
sell v vendre
seminar le séminaire
send v envoyer
senior citizens les seniors
separated (marriage) séparés
serious sérieux
service (in a restaurant) le service
sexually transmitted disease (STD) les maladies sexuellement transmissibles
shampoo le shampooing
sharp tranchant
shaving cream la mousse à raser
sheet le drap
shirt la chemise
ship v envoyer
shoe store le magasin de chaussures
shoes les chaussures
shop v faire des achats
shopping les courses;

~**area** le quartier des magasins; ~**centre [BE]** le centre commercial; ~**mall** le centre commercial
short court; ~**-sighted [BE]** myope; ~**sleeves** les manches courtes; ~**s** le short
shoulder l'épaule
show v montrer
shower la douche
shrine le lieu saint
sick malade
side dish l'accompagnement
side effect l'effet secondaire
sightseeing le tourisme; ~**tour** la visite touristique
sign v signer
silk la soie
single (unmarried) adj célibataire; n ~**bed** le lit une place; ~**prints** le tirage unique; ~**room** la chambre simple
sink l'évier
sister la sœur
sit v s'asseoir
size la taille
ski v skier; ~n le ski; ~**lift** le télésiège
skin la peau
skirt la jupe
sleep v dormir
sleeper car le wagon couchette

sleeping bag le sac de couchage

sleeping car [BE] le wagon couchette

slice la tranche

slippers les chaussons

slower plus lent

slowly lentement

small petit

smaller plus petit

smoke v fumer

smoking (area) la zone fumeur

snack bar le bar

sneakers les tennis

snorkeling equipment l'équipement de plongée

snowboard le snowboard

snowshoe la chaussure de ski

snowy neigeux

soap le savon

soccer le football; ~**game** le match de football

sock la chaussette

soother [BE] la tétine

sore throat le mal de gorge

sorry désolé

south sud

souvenir le souvenir; ~**store** le magasin de souvenirs

spa le spa

spatula la spatule

speak v parler

special (food) la spécialité; le plat typique

specialist (doctor) le spécialiste

specimen l'échantillon

speed (velocity) la vitesse

spell v épeler

spicy épicé

spine (body part) la colonne vertébrale

spoon la cuillère

sporting goods store le magasin de sport

sports le sport; ~**massage** le massage sportif

sprain l'entorse

stadium le stade

stairs les escaliers

stamp v (a ticket) timbrer; ~n (postage) le timbre

start v (a car) démarrer; v (to begin) commencer

starter [BE] l'entrée

station la station; ~**wagon** le break; **bus** ~ la gare routière; **gas** ~ la station service; **muster** ~[BE] la salle d'attente; **petrol** ~[BE] la station service; **subway** ~ la station de métro; **train** ~ la gare

statue la statue

stay v rester

steal v voler

steep escarpé

sterling silver l'argent fin

sting la piqûre
stolen volé
stomach l'estomac;
~**ache** les maux de ventre
stop v arrêter; ~n l'arrêt
store directory le plan du
magasin
stove la gazinière
straight droit
strange étrange
stream le ruisseau
stroller la poussette
student l'étudiant
study v étudier
stunning stupéfiant
subtitle subtil
subway le métro; ~**station** la
station de métro
suit le costume; ~**case** la
valise
sun le soleil; ~**block** l'écran
solaire; ~**burn** le coup de
soleil; ~**glasses** les lunettes
de soleil
sunny ensoleillé
sunscreen la crème solaire
sunstroke l'insolation
super (fuel) le super;
~**market** le supermarché;
~**vision** la supervision
surfboard le surf
swallow v avaler
sweater le pull
sweatshirt le sweat-shirt
sweet (taste) sucré

sweets [BE] les bonbons
swell v gonfler
swim v nager
swimsuit le maillot de bain
symbol (keyboard) le
symbole
synagogue la synagogue

T

table la table
tablet (medicine) le cachet
take v prendre
take away [BE] à emporter
tampon le tampon
taste v goûter
taxi le taxi
team l'équipe
teaspoon la cuillère à café
telephone le téléphone
temple (religious) le temple
temporary temporaire
tennis le tennis
tent la tente; ~**peg** le piquet;
~**pole** le pilier
terminal (airport) le terminal
terracotta la terre cuite
terrible terrible
text v (send a
message) écrire; ~n
(message) le texte
thank v remercier;
~**you** merci
that ça/cela
theater le théâtre
theft le vol

there là
thief le voleur
thigh la cuisse
thirsty soif
this ceci
throat la gorge
ticket le billet; **~office** la billetterie
tie (clothing) la cravate
time le temps; **~table** [BE] les horaires
tire [tyre BE] le pneu
tired fatigué
tissues les Kleenex
to go aller
tobacconist le tabac
today aujourd'hui
toe l'orteil; **~nail** l'ongle
toilet [BE] les toilettes; **~paper** le papier toilette
tomorrow demain
tongue la langue
tonight ce soir
too trop
tooth la dent; **~paste** le dentifrice
total (amount) le total
tough (food) dur
tour la visite
tourist le touriste; **~information office** le syndicat d'initiative
tow truck la dépanneuse
towel la serviette
tower la tour

town la ville; **~hall** la mairie; **~map** la carte de la ville; **~square** le centre ville
toy le jouet; **~store** le magasin de jouets
track (train) le quai
traditional traditionnel
traffic light le feu tricolore
trail la piste; **~map** la carte des pistes
trailer la remorque
train le train; **~station** la gare
translate *v* traduire
trash les poubelles
travel *v* voyager; **~agency** l'agence de voyage; **~sickness** le mal des transports; **~er's check [cheque BE]** le chèque de voyages
tree l'arbre
trim (hair cut) *v* égaliser
trip le voyage
trolley [BE] le chariot
trousers [BE] le pantalon
T-shirt le t-shirt
turn off *v* **(lights)** éteindre
turn on *v* **(lights)** allumer
TV la télé
type *v* taper

U

ugly laid
umbrella le parapluie
unattended sans surveillance

unbranded medication [BE] le médicament générique

unconscious inconscient

underground [BE] le métro; **~station [BE]** la station de métro

underpants [BE] les slips

understand *v* comprendre

underwear les sous-vêtements

United Kingdom (U.K.) le Royaume Uni

United States (U.S.) les États-Unis

university l'université

unleaded (gas) sans plomb

upper supérieur

urgent urgent

use *v* utiliser

username le nom de l'utilisateur

utensil l'ustensile

V

vacancy libre

vacation les vacances

vaccination la vaccination

vacuum cleaner l'aspirateur

vagina le vagin

vaginal infection l'infection vaginale

valid valide

valley la vallée

valuable précieux

value la valeur

VAT [BE] la TVA

vegetarian végétarien

vehicle registration la carte grise

viewpoint [BE] le point d'observation

village le village

vineyard le vignoble

visit *v* visiter; **~ing hours** les heures de visite

visually impaired le malvoyant

vitamin la vitamine

V-neck le col en V

volleyball game le match de volleyball

vomit *v* vomir

W

wait *v* attendre; **~n** l'attente

waiter le serveur

waiting room la salle d'attente

waitress la serveuse

wake *v* réveiller; **~-up call** *n* l'appel réveil

walk *v* marcher; **~n** la promenade; **~ing route** le chemin de randonnée

wall clock la pendule

wallet le portefeuille

warm (something) *v* réchauffer **~** *adj*

(temperature) chaud
washing machine la machine
à laver
watch la montre
water skis les skis nautiques
waterfall la cascade
weather le temps
week la semaine; **~week-
end** le week-end
weekly hebdomadaire
welcome v accueillir
well-rested bien reposé
west ouest
what quoi
wheelchair la chaise
roulante; **~ramp** la rampe
d'accès
when quand
where où
white blanc; **~gold** l'or blanc
who qui
widow le veuf
wife l'épouse
window la fenêtre; **~case** le
chambranle
windsurfer le véliplanchiste
wine list la carte des vins

wireless internet l'accès
Wi-Fi
wireless phone le portable
with avec
withdraw v retirer
withdrawal (bank) le retrait
without sans
woman la femme
wool la laine
work v travailler
wrap v emballer
wrist le poignet
write v écrire

Y

year l'année
yellow jaune; **~gold** l'or jaune
yes oui
yesterday hier
you're welcome de rien
young jeune
youth hostel l'auberge de
jeunesse

Z

zoo le zoo

FRENCH–ENGLISH

A

à droite right (direction)
à gauche left (direction)
l'abbaye abbey
abîmer v damage
accéder v access
accepter v accept
l'accès Wi-Fi wireless internet
accessible aux handicapés handicapped-[disabled- BE] accessible
l'accident accident
l'accompagnement side dish
d'accord OK
accueillir v welcome
acheter v buy
l'acuponcture acupuncture
l'adaptateur adapter
l'addition bill (check)
l'adresse address; ~ **mail** e-mail address
l'aéroport airport
les affaires business
l'âge age
l'agence agency; ~ **de voyage** travel agency
l'aide n help
aider v help
aimer v like (someone); ~ v love (someone)
l'aire de jeux playground; ~ **de sport** field (sports)

l'aire de pique-nique picnic area
allaiter v breastfeed
l'allée aisle (theater)
aller v go (somewhere)
l'aller simple one-way (ticket)
allergique allergic; ~ **au lactose** lactose intolerant
l'aller-retour round-trip [return BE]
allumer v light (cigarette); ~ v turn on (lights)
l'ambulance ambulance
américain American
l'ami friend
amour n love
l'ampoule lightbulb
anémique anemic
l'anesthésie anesthesia
anglais British; English
l'animal animal
l'année year
l'anniversaire birthday
annuler v cancel
l'antibiotique antibiotic
l'antiquaire antique store
l'appareil photo camera; ~ **numérique** digital camera
l'appartement apartment
l'appel phone call
appeler v call
l'appendice appendix (body

part)

apporter v bring

après after

l'après after;

~ **-midi** afternoon;

~ **-rasage** aftershave;

~ **-shampooing** conditioner

l'arbre tree

la salle de jeux arcade

l'argent money; ~ **fin** sterling
silver

l'aromathérapie
aromatherapy

arracher v extract (tooth)

l'arrêt n stop; ~ **de bus** bus
stop

arrêter v stop

les arrivées arrivals (airport)

arriver v arrive

l'art arts

l'artère artery

l'arthrite arthritis

l'articulation joint (body part)

l'ascenseur elevator [lift BE]

asiatique Asian

l'aspirateur vacuum cleaner

l'aspirine aspirin

l'assiette plate

l'assurance insurance

asthmatique asthmatic

l'attaque attack

attaquer v mug

atteindre v reach

attendre v wait

l'attente n wait

au coin on/around the corner

au revoir goodbye

l'auberge de jeunesse youth
hostel

aujourd'hui today

l'Australie Australia

australien Australian

automatique automatic

l'autoroute highway
[motorway BE]

avaler v swallow

l'avance cash advance

avant before

avec with

l'avion airplane

l'avocat lawyer

avoir v have; ~ **besoin** v
need; ~ **des vertiges** dizzy;
~ **la nausée** nauseous; ~ **un
accident** v crash (car)

B

le baby-sitter babysitter

le bagage à main carry-on
[piece of hand luggage BE]

le bagage luggage [baggage
BE]

la bague ring

les baguettes chopsticks

le balai broom

le ballet ballet

la banque bank

le bar bar (place), snack bar;
~ **gay** gay bar

le barbecue barbecue

la barque rowboat
bas low
le baseball baseball
le basketball basketball
le bateau boat; **~ à moteur** motor boat
le bâtiment building
les bâtons poles (skiing)
beau attractive, beautiful
le bébé baby
le bed and breakfast bed and breakfast
beige beige
belle pretty
le berceau crib
le biberon baby bottle
la bibliothèque library
la bicyclette bicycle
bien well; **~ reposé** well-rested
le bijou jewelry
la bijouterie jeweler
le bikini bikini
la billeterie ticket office; **~ électronique** e-ticket
blanc white
bleu blue
boire v drink
la boisson n drink
la boîte box; **~ -à-lettres** mailbox [postbox BE]
bon adj good; **~ après-midi** good afternoon; **~marché** cheap
le bonbon candy [sweet BE]

bonjour hello, good morning
bonsoir good evening
les bottes boots
la bouche mouth
le boucher butcher
les boucles d'oreille earrings
la boulangerie bakery
la bouteille bottle
la boutique photo camera store
le bracelet bracelet
le bras arm
le briquet lighter
la broche brooch
la brosse hairbrush
brûler v burn
la buanderie laundry facility
le bureau office; **~ de change** currency exchange office; **~ de poste** post office; **~ des renseignements** information desk; **~ de réservation** reservation desk
le bus bus; **~ direct** express bus

C

ça that
le cabaret cabaret
la cabine cabin; **~ d'essayage** fitting [changing BE] room
le cachet tablet (medicine)
le cadeau gift

le cadenas *n* lock
le café café, coffee shop
la caisse cashier
les kilocalories calories
camper *v* camp
le camping campsite
le Canada Canada
canadien Canadian
la carafe carafe
le carrousel conveyor belt
la carte map, card;
  ~ d'assurance insurance
  card;
  ~ des boissons drink menu;
  ~ de la chambre key card;
  ~ de crédit credit card;
  ~ d'embarquement
  boarding pass;
  ~ internationale d'étudiant
  international student card;
  ~ grise vehicle registration;
  ~ de membre membership
  card;
  ~ mémoire memory card;
  ~ des pistes trail [piste BE]
  map;
  ~ postale postcard;
  ~ de retrait ATM/debit card;
  ~ routière road map;
  ~ de téléphone phone card;
  ~ de la ville town map;
  ~ de visite business card
la carte des vins wine list
la cartouche (de cigarettes)
  carton (of cigarettes)

le cas case (amount)
la cascade waterfall
le casino casino
le casque helmet
cassé broken
casser *v* break (tooth, bone)
la casserole pot, saucepan
la cathédrale cathedral
la cave cave, cellar (wine)
le CD (disque compact) CD
ce soir tonight
ceci this
la ceinture belt
cela that
célibataire single (unmarried)
le cellophane plastic wrap
  [cling film BE]
Celsius Celsius
le centimètre centimeter
centre center; **~ commercial**
  shopping mall [centre BE];
  ~ d'affaires business
  center; **~ ville** town square;
  ~ -ville downtown area
le certificat certificate
la chaîne key ring, chain
la chaise chair;
  ~ haute highchair;
  ~ longue deck chair;
  ~ roulante wheelchair
le chambranle display
  window/case
la chambre simple single
  room
le champ field; **~ de bataille**

battleground; ~ **la piste de course** horsetrack

le change *n* exchange (place)

changer *v* change (baby)

le chapeau hat

le charbon de bois charcoal

la charcuterie delicatessen

le chariot cart [trolley BE]

le château castle

chaud hot, warm (temperature)

le chauffage heat (indoor)

le chauffage heater

la chaussette sock

les chaussons slippers

les chaussures shoes; ~ **de ski** snowshoes; ~ **à talons aiguilles** high-heeled shoes; ~ **de marche** hiking boots; ~ **plates** flat shoes

le chemin trail, path; ~ **de randonnée** walking route

la chemise shirt

le chemisier blouse

le chèque *n* check [cheque BE] (payment); ~ **de voyages** traveler's check [cheque BE]

cher expensive

les cheveux hair

la cheville ankle

le chewing-gum chewing gum

le chien d'aveugle guide dog

chinois Chinese

le cigare cigar

la cigarette cigarette

le cinéma movie theater

les ciseaux scissors

la classe class; ~ **affaire** business class; ~ **économique** economy class

la clé key

la climatisation air conditioning

le club club; ~ **gay** gay club; ~ **de jazz** jazz club

le code code; ~ **national** country code; ~ **régional** area code; ~ **secret** personal identification number (PIN)

le cœur heart

le coffre-fort safe (receptacle)

le coiffeur hair salon

le coiffeur pour hommes barber

le col rond crew neck

le col en V *V* V-neck

le colis package

le collègue colleague

le collier necklace

la colline hill

la colonne vertébrale spine (body part)

combien how much

commander *v* order

commencer *v* begin

comment how

le commissariat de police police station

la compagnie aérienne
airline

la compagnie d'assurance
insurance company

composer v dial

comprendre v understand

le compte account; ~ **courant**
checking [current BE]
account; ~ **épargne** savings
account

le concert concert

conduire v drive

la conférence conference

confirmer v confirm

le congélateur freezer

la congestion congestion

se connecter v connect
(internet)

la connexion connection
(internet, telephone)

les conserves canned goods

la consigne luggage locker

la consigne locker

constipé constipated

le consulat consulate

le consultant consultant

contacter v contact

contagieux contagious

le contraire opposite

la contravention fine (fee for
breaking law)

le contrôle de passeport
passport control

la correspondance change
(buses); ~ connection (flight);

~ v transfer (change trains/
flights)

le costume suit

la côte rib (body part)

le coton cotton

la couche diaper [nappy BE]

la couchette berth

le coude elbow

la couleur color

le couloir aisle (plane)

le cou neck

le coup de soleil sunburn

couper v cut

la coupure bill [note BE]
(money); ~ cut (injury)

le courrier mail [post BE];
~ **recommandé** registered
mail

court short

le coût charge (cost)

le couteau knife

coûter v cost

le couvert cover charge
(restaurant)

la couverture blanket

la cravate tie (clothing)

la crème cream/lotion;
~ **antiseptique** antiseptic
cream; ~ **solaire** sunscreen

le cristal crystal

la cuillère spoon; ~ **à café**
teaspoon; ~ **à doser**
measuring spoon

le cuir leather

la cuisine kitchen

cuisiner v cook
la cuisse thigh
le cuivre copper
les culottes panties
le cyber café internet café

D

dangereux dangerous
dans in
dansant dancing
danser v dance
la date date (calendar)
de nuit overnight
de rien you're welcome
le **déboucheur de
toilettes** plunger
le débutant beginner
déclarer v declare
décoller v take off (plane)
déconnecter disconnect
  (computer)
le degré degree (temperature)
dehors outside
le déjeuner lunch
délicieux delicious
demain tomorrow
démarrer v start (an
  automobile)
demi half; ~ **-heure** half hour;
  ~ **-kilo** half-kilo
la dent tooth
la dentelle lace
le dentier denture
le dentifrice toothpaste
le dentiste dentist

le déodorant deodorant
la dépanneuse tow truck
les départs departures
  (airport)
déposer v deposit
le dépôt deposit (bank)
dernier last
derrière behind
descendre v get off (a train,
  bus, subway)
le désert desert
désolé sorry
le détergent detergent;
  ~ **pour lave-vaisselle**
  dishwashing liquid
développer v develop (film)
la déviation alternate route
diabétique diabetic
le diamant diamond
la diarrhée diarrhea
difficile difficult
dîner v dine; **le** ~ dinner
la direction direction
la discothèque dance club;
disparu missing
disponible available
le disquaire music store
**le distributeur automatique
  de billets** automatic teller
  machine (ATM)
le divertissement
  entertainment
divorcer v divorce
le docteur doctor
le doigt finger

le dollar dollar (U.S.)
donner v give
dormir v sleep
le dortoir dormitory
le dos back (body part)
la douane customs
doublé dubbed
la douche shower
la douleur hurt, pain;
~ **à la poitrine** chest pain
la douzaine dozen
le drap sheet
droit straight;
~ **d'entrée** cover charge
(bar, club)
du quartier local
DVD DVD

E

l'eau water; ~ **chaude**
hot water; ~ **de**
Cologne cologne;
~ **potable** drinking water
l'échange de monnaie
currency exchange
échanger v change (money)
l'échantillon specimen
l'écharpe scarf
l'école school
les écouteurs headphones
l'écran solaire sunblock
écrire v text (send a
message); ~ v write
effacer v clear (on an ATM)
l'effet secondaire side effect

l'effraction break-in (burglary)
égaliser trim (hair cut)
l'église church
l'émail enamel (jewelry)
emballer v wrap
embarquer v board
embrasser v kiss
emporter to go [take away BE]
(food order)
en sécurité safe (protected)
encaisser v cash
enceinte pregnant
endommagé damaged
l'enfant child
enlacer v hug
ennuyant boring
l'enregistrement check-in
(hotel, airport)
enregistrer v check (luggage)
ensoleillé sunny
l'entorse sprain
l'entrée admission;
~ appetizer [starter BE];
~ entrance
entrer v enter
l'enveloppe envelope
envoyer v send, ship; ~ **un**
fax v fax; ~ **un mail** v e-mail
l'épaule shoulder
épeler v spell
épicé hot (spicy)
l'épilation à la cire du
maillot bikini wax
l'épilation à la cire des
sourcils eyebrow wax

épileptique epileptic
l'épouse wife
épuisé exhausted
l'équipe team
l'équipement equipment;
~ **de plongée** diving/
snorkeling equipment
l'erreur mistake
l'escalator escalators
les escaliers stairs
escarpé steep
ennuyer v bother
l'essence gas
l'essence petrol
est east
l'esthéticienne manicurist
l'estomac stomach
et and
l'étain pewter
l'étang pond
l'état de santé condition
(medical); ~ **le problème
cardiaque** heart condition
les États-Unis United States
(U.S.)
éteindre v turn off (lights)
l'étiquette baggage ticket
étrange strange
être v be
l'étudiant student
étudier v study
l'euro euro
l'éventail fan (souvenir)
l'évier sink
l'excès excess

l'excursion excursion
excuser v excuse
l'expert expert (skill level)
l'express express
extra extra

F

facile easy
la facture bill [invoice BE]
faim hungry
faire v make, do; ~ **des
achats** v shop; ~ **de l'auto
stop** v hitchhike; ~ **les
bagages** v pack; ~ **les
courses** shopping; ~ **le
plein** v fill; **se ~ réveiller
par téléphone** wake-up call;
~ **du tourisme** sightseeing;
~ **du vélo** cycling; ~ **de la
vitesse** speeding
faire un virement v transfer
(money)
la falaise cliff
la famille family
le fast-food fast food
fatigué tired
le fax fax
la femme woman
la fenêtre window
le fer à repasser n iron
(clothes)
fermé closed
la ferme farm
fermer v close, lock
le ferry ferry

les fesses buttocks
le feu fire; ~ **tricolore** traffic light
fiancé engaged
la fièvre fever
la fille girl
le film movie
finir v end
la fleur flower
le foie liver (body part)
la fontaine fountain
le football soccer [football BE]
la forêt forest; ~ **vierge** rainforest
le forfait lift pass
le formulaire form
le fort fort
la fourchette fork
frais cool (temperature); ~ fresh
français French
la France France
frapper v (computer) type
les freins brakes (car)
le frère brother
froid cold (temperature)
fumer v smoke

G

le garage garage, parking garage
garer v park
le garçon boy
la gare train [railway BE] station
la gare routière bus station
gay gay
le gaz cooking gas
la gazinière stove
le gazole diesel
le gel gel (hair)
le genou knee
le gilet de sauvetage life jacket
glacé icy
la glace ice
gonfler v swell
la gorge canyon; ~ throat
goûter v taste
la goutte drop (medicine)
le gramme gram
grand large
le grand magasin department store
grande taille plus size
les grands-parents grandparent
graver v engrave
gris gray
le groupe group
la gueule de bois hangover
le guide guide, guidebook
la gym gym
le gynécologue gynecologist

H

l'handicapé handicapped [disabled BE]
haut high

hebdomadaire weekly
l'hectare hectare
l'hétérosexuel heterosexual
l'heure hour
les heures d'ouverture business/office hours
les heures de visite visiting hours
heureux happy
hier yesterday
le hockey hockey; ~ **sur glace** ice hockey
l'homme man
l'hôpital hospital
l'horaire schedule [timetable BE]
hors taxe duty-free
l'hôtel hotel
l'huile oil

I

l'ibuprofène ibuprofen
ici here
l'identification identification
l'imperméable raincoat
imprimer v print
inclure v include
inconscient unconscious
infecté infected
l'infection vaginale vaginal infection
l'infirmier nurse
informer v notify
l'insecte bug
insérer v insert

l'insolation sunstroke
l'insomnie insomnia
l'insuline insulin
interdire v prohibit
intéressant interesting
l'international (terminal) international (airport area)
l'internet internet; ~ **sans fil** wireless internet
l'interprète interpreter
l'intersection intersection
l'intestin intestine
irlandais Irish
l'Irlande Ireland
l'irritation cutanée rash
italien Italian

J

la jambe leg
le jardin botanique botanical garden
jaune yellow
le jazz jazz
le jean jeans
jean denim
jetable disposable
le jeu game
jeune young
joindre v join
jouer v play
le jouet toy
le jour day
le journal newspaper
la jupe skirt

K

le kilo kilo;
~**gramme** kilogram;
~**métrage** mileage;
~**mètre** kilometer; ~**mètre carré** square kilometer
le kiosque à journaux newsstand
les Kleenex tissue

L

le lac lake
laid ugly
la laine wool
le lait pour bébés formula (baby)
la lame de rasoir razor blade
la lampe torche flashlight
la langue tongue
la laque hairspray
la laverie automatique laundromat [launderette BE]
le lave-vaisselle dishwasher
la leçon lesson
lentement slowly
les lentilles de contact contact lens
la lessive laundry
la lettre letter
les lèvres lip
la librairie bookstore
libre free; ~ **vacancy**
le lieu n place;
~ **commémoratif** memorial
(place); ~ **saint** shrine;
~ **touristique** attraction (place)
la ligne line (train)
la lime à ongle nail file
la lingette pour bébé baby wipe
le lin linen
le liquide n cash
le lit bed; ~ **double** double bed; ~ **pliant** cot
le litre liter
le livre book
la livre sterling pounds (British sterling)
le logement accommodation
loin far
long long
la lotion anti-insectes insect repellent
louer v rent [hire BE]
la lumière light (overhead)
les lunettes glasses; ~ **de soleil** sunglasses

M

la machine à laver washing machine
la mâchoire jaw
le magasin store;
~ **de chaussures** shoe store;
~ **de jouets** toy store;
~ **de produits diététiques** health food store;

~ de souvenirs souvenir store **~ de sport** sporting goods store; **~ de vêtements** clothing store; **~ de vins et spiritueux** liquor store
le magazine magazine
magnifique magnificent
le mail e-mail
le maillot de bain swimsuit
la main hand
maintenant now
la maison house
le mal sickness; **~ de l'air** motion-sickness (air); **~ de dos** backache; **~ de gorge** sore throat; **~ de mer** motion sickness (sea); **~ de tête** headache; **~ des transports** travel sickness
malade ill, sick
les maladies sexuellement transmissibles sexually transmitted disease (STD)
malvoyant visually impaired
les manches courtes short sleeves
les manches longues long sleeves
manger v eat
le manteau coat
la manucure manicure
le marchand de fruits et légumes produce store
le marchand de vins et de

spiritueux liquor store [off-licence BE]
le marché market
marcher v walk
le mari husband
marié married
la mairie town hall
se marier v marry
marron brown
le marteau hammer
le massage massage
le match n match; **~ de boxe** boxing match; **~ de football** soccer [football BE] game; **~ de volleyball** volleyball game
le matin morning
le maux de ventre stomachache
le mécanicien mechanic
le médicament medicine
meilleur best
le même same
le menu menu; **~ enfant** children's menu
la mer sea
merci thank you
la mère mother
le message message; **~ instantané** instant message
la messe mass (church service)
la mesure measuring cup
mesurer to measure

(someone)

la météo forecast

le mètre carré square meter

le métro subway [underground BE]

le micro-onde microwave

midi noon [midday BE]

mieux better

mignon cute

le mini bar mini-bar

minuit midnight

la minute minute

le mobile home mobile home

la mobilité mobility

la mobylette moped

les mocassins loafers

modifier v alter

moins less; ~ **cher** cheaper

le mois month

la moitié half

la monnaie n change (money); ~ currency

la montagne mountain

la montre watch

montrer v show

le morceau piece

la mosquée mosque

le mot de passe password

la moto motorcycle

la mousse mousse; ~ **à raser** shaving cream

moyen medium (size)

le muscle muscle

le musée museum

la musique music;

~ **classique** classical music; ~ **folklorique** folk music

myope near- [short- BE] sighted

N

nager v swim

national domestic

la nationalité nationality

neigeux snowy

nettoyer v clean

le nez nose

le night club nightclub

le niveau intermédiaire intermediate

noir black

le nom name; ~ **de l'utilisateur** username

non no; ~ **alcoolisé** non-alcoholic; ~ **fumeur** non-smoking

nord north

nourrir v feed

le novice novice (skill level)

de nuit overnight

la nuit night

numérique digital

le numéro number; ~ **de fax** fax number; ~ **de permis de conduire** driver's license -number; ~ **de téléphone** phone number

O

les objets trouvés lost and found

l'œil eye

l'oiseau bird

l'ongle fingernail, toenail

l'opéra opera

l'opticien optician

l'or gold; **~ blanc** white gold; **~ jaune** yellow gold

orange orange (color)

l'orchestre orchestra

ordinaire regular

l'ordinateur computer

l'ordonnance prescription

les ordures à recycler recycling

l'oreille ear

l'oreiller pillow

l'orteil toe

l'os bone

l'otite earache

où where

ouest west

oui yes

ouvert open

l'ouvre-bouteille/ boîte bottle/can opener

ouvrir v open; **~ une session** v log on (computer)

P

le palais palace

le palais des congrès -convention hall

le panier basket (grocery store)

la panne breakdown

le pansement bandage

le pantalon pants [trousers BE]

le papier paper; **~ aluminium** aluminum [kitchen BE] foil; **~ toilette** toilet paper

le paquet carton

par by; **~ avion** airmail; **~ heure** per hour; **~ jour** per day; **~ nuit** per night; **~ semaine** per week

le paracétamol acetaminophen [paracetamol BE]

le parapluie umbrella

le parc playpen; **~** park; **~ d'attractions** amusement park

le parfum perfume

parier to place (a bet)

le parking parking lot [car park BE]

parler v speak

participer v attend

pas cher inexpensive

le passager passenger

le passeport passport

passer v pass through

la passoire colander

la pataugeoire kiddie pool

la pâtisserie pastry shop

payer *v* pay; **~ par carte** *v* charge (credit card)

la peau skin

le pédiatre pediatrician

la pédicure pedicure

le peigne comb

la pellicule film (camera)

pendant during

la pendule wall clock

la pénicilline penicillin

le pénis penis

perdre *v* lose (something)

perdu lost

le père father

la période period (of time)

la perle pearl

permettre *v* allow

la perte discharge (bodily fluid)

petit small

le petit child, small; **~ -ami** boyfriend; **~ -amie** girlfriend; **~ déjeuner** breakfast

les petits-enfants grandchildren

peu little

la pharmacie pharmacy [chemist BE]

la photo photo; **~copie** photocopy; **~graphie** photography; **~ numérique** digital photo

la pièce coin; **~ part** (for car); **~** *n* play (theater); **~ room**

le pied foot

le piéton pedestrian

la pile battery

le pilier tent pole

la pilule Pill (birth control)

le piquet tent peg

la piqûre sting; **~ d'insecte** insect bite

la piscine pool; **~ intérieure** indoor pool; **~ extérieure** outdoor pool

la piste trail [piste BE]; **~ cyclable** bike route

la pizzeria pizzeria

la plage beach

la plainte complaint

le plaisir pleasure

le plan du magasin store directory

le plat principal main course

platine platinum

le plombage filling (tooth)

plonger *v* dive

la pluie rain

plus more; **~ bas** lower; **~ fort** louder; **~ grand** larger; **~ lent** slower; **~ petit** smaller; **~ tard** later; **~ tôt** earlier; **~ vite** faster

pluvieux rainy

le pneu tire [tyre BE]; **~ crevé** flat tire [tyre BE]

la poche pocket

la poêle frying pan

le poignet wrist

le point d'observation overlook [viewpoint BE] (scenic place)

le poison poison

la poitrine chest (body part)

la police police

la pompe à air air pump

les pompiers fire department

le pont bridge

la pop musique pop music

le portable wireless/cell [mobile BE] phone

la porte gate (airport); ~ door; ~ **coupe-feu** fire door

le portefeuille wallet

la portion portion; ~ **enfant** children's portion

la pose exposure (film)

le poste extension (phone)

le pot jar

la poterie pottery

le poubelle garbage [rubbish BE]

le poumon lung

la poupée doll

pour for

pourpre purple

pousser to push (door sign)

la poussette stroller [pushchair BE]

précieux valuable

premier first

la première classe first class

prendre v pick up (something); ~ v take; ~ **plaisir** v enjoy; ~ **sa retraite** retired

près close, near; ~ **de** nearby

presbyte far- [long- BE] sighted

prescrire to prescribe

présenter v introduce

le préservatif condom

prévoir v schedule

la principale attraction touristique main attraction

la prise électrique electric outlet

le prix price

le problème problem

produire produce

le produit product; ~ **d'entretien** cleaning product; ~ **ménager** household good

profondément deeply

la promenade walk

prononcer v pronounce

propre clean

public public

le pull sweater

le pyjama pajamas

Q

le quai n track [platform BE] (train)

la qualité quality

quand when

le quartier des magasins
shopping area
la question question
qui who
quitter la chambre check-out
(hotel)
quoi what

R

raccourcir v to shorten
la rampe d'accès wheelchair
ramp
le rap rap (music)
le rapport de police police
report
la raquette racket (sports)
le rasoir jetable disposable
razor
la réaction allergique allergic
reaction
la réception reception
recevoir v receive
recharger v recharge
le réchaud camping stove
réchauffer v warm
(something)
recommandation
recommendation
recommander v recommend
le reçu n bill, receipt (of sale)
recycler recycling
la réduction discount
le réfrigérateur refrigerator
refuser v decline (credit card)
regarder v look

la région region
les règles period (menstrual)
les règles douloureuses
menstrual cramps
le rein kidney (body part)
la relation relationship
remercier v thank
le remonte-pentes drag lift
la remorque trailer
remplir v fill out (form)
rencontrer v meet (someone)
le rendez-vous appointment
rendre v return (something)
les renseignements
information (phone)
réparer v fix (repair)
le repas meal
repasser v iron
répéter v repeat
la réservation reservation
la réserve naturelle nature
preserve
réserver v reserve
le résident européen EU
resident
respirer v breathe
le responsable manager
le restaurant restaurant
rester v stay
retarder v delay
retirer v withdraw
le retrait withdrawal (bank);
~ des bagages baggage
claim
la réunion meeting

réveiller v wake
le rez-de-chaussée ground floor
le rhume cold (sickness)
rien anything, nothing
la rivière river
la robe dress (piece of clothing)
romantique romantic
rose pink
rouge red
la route route
le Royaume Uni United Kingdom (U.K.)
le rugby rugby
les ruines ruins
le ruisseau stream

S

s'asseoir v sit
s'il vous plaît please
le sac bag, purse; ~à dos backpack; ~ à appareil photo camera case; ~ de couchage sleeping bag; ~ à main purse [handbag BE]; ~ poubelle garbage [rubbish BE] bag
le sachet bag
saigner v bleed
le saladier bowl
sale dirty
la salle room:
  ~ d'attente waiting room;
  ~ de concert concert hall;
  ~ à manger dining room;
  ~ de réunion meeting room
le salon d'essayage fitting room
salut hi
les sandales sandals
le sang blood
sans without; ~ 0% de matières
~ **grasses** fat free;
  ~ **ordonnance** over the counter (medication);
  ~ **plomb** unleaded (gasoline);
  ~ **surveillance** unattended
la santé health
Santé! Cheers!
le sauna sauna
sauvegarder v save (computer)
le savon soap
le scanner scanner
la science science
le sèche-cheveux hair dryer
le secouriste lifeguard
la sécurité security
le sein breast
le self-service self-service
la semaine week
le séminaire seminar
les seniors senior citizens
le sens unique one-way street
séparé separated (marriage)
sérieux serious

la serpillière mop;
~ groundcloth
le serveur waiter
la serveuse waitress
le service service (in a
restaurant);
~ de chambre room service;
~ complet full-service;
~ d'entretien housekeeping
services; ~ internet internet
service; ~ de nettoyage
laundry service
la serviette napkin, towel;
~ hygiénique sanitary
napkin [pad BE]
seul alone
seulement only
le shampooing shampoo
le short shorts
le siège seat; ~ bébé car
seat; ~ couloir aisle seat;
~ enfant child's seat
signer v sign
le silence quiet
le ski ski; ~ jet jet ski
skier v ski
les skis nautiques water skis
les slips briefs [underpants
BE] (clothing)
le snowboard snowboard
la sœur sister
la soie silk
soif thirsty
le soin à l'oxygène oxygen
treatment

le soin du visage facial
la soirée evening
le sol floor
le soleil sun
la solution pour lentilles
de contact contact lens
solution
sombre dark
le sommet peak
somnolence drowsiness
la serviette en papier paper
towel
la sortie exit; ~ de secours
emergency exit
sortir to exit
la source chaude hot spring
sourd deaf
les sous-vêtements
underwear
le soutien-gorge bra
le souvenir souvenir
le spa spa
la spatule spatula
le spécialiste specialist
(doctor)
le sport sports
le stade stadium
la station station; ~ de
métro subway [underground
BE] station; ~ service gas
[petrol BE] station
la statue statue
stupéfiant stunning
le style de coiffure hairstyle
le stylo pen

subtil subtitle
sucré sweet (taste)
sud south
suivant next
le super super (fuel)
supérieur upper
le supermarché supermarket
la supervision supervision
supprimer v delete
  (computer)
le surf surfboard
surprenant amazing
le sweat-shirt sweatshirt
le symbole symbol (keyboard)
la synagogue synagogue
le syndicat d'initiative tourist
  information office
**le Syndrome
  d'immunodéficience
  acquise (SIDA)** AIDS

T

le tabac tobacconist
la table table
la taille size
le tampon tampon
le tapis de sol groundcloth
tard late (time)
la tasse cup
le taux de change exchange
  rate
la taxe duty (tax)
le taxi taxi
la teinturerie dry cleaner
la télé TV; **~le téléphérique**

cable car; **~le téléphone**
phone; **~le téléphone public**
pay phone
téléphoner v phone
le télésiège chair lift
le temple temple (religious)
temporaire temporary
le temps time, weather;
  ~ partiel part-time;
  ~ plein full-time
le tennis tennis
les tennis sneakers
la tension blood pressure
la tente tent
la tenue exigée dress code
le terminal terminal (airport)
terminer une session v log
  off (computer)
le terrain field, course; **~ de
  golf** golf course
la terre cuite terracotta
terrible terrible
la tête head (body part)
la tétine pacifier [soother BE]
le texte text (message)
le théâtre theater
le ticket ticket; **~ de bus** bus
  ticket
le timbre stamp (postage)
le tirage unique single prints
le tire-bouchon corkscrew
tirer v pull (door sign)
les toilettes restroom [toilet
  BE]